Kristen's words will comfort your heart, care for your soul, and always, always carry you toward the hope of Christ. Through her writing that is both beautiful and truthful, you'll learn how to lean into the love of God when suffering threatens to hide your view of his goodness. May her words buoy you in whatever storm you're facing.

PHYLICIA MASONHEIMER, Founder and CEO of Every Woman a Theologian

Trauma ignites so many different emotions in each of us, but the last thing we need is to feel like a failure because our faith feels shaky. Kristen mirrors courageous, raw honesty as she helps you flip the script on the way suffering has tutored you to how God *actually* talks about suffering on the pages of Scripture. Kristen is a gifted storyteller—you will not want to put this book down. No empty platitudes or pithy sayings here, just real-life examples of how to apply the Bible to your current suffering.

MIKELLA VAN DYKE, Author and founder of Chasing Sacred

As I joined the whole internet praying and rallying around the LaValley family in 2020, I had no idea that Kristen's words about their experience would later help bind up deep wounds tied to my own grief and tragedy. Many books talk about Christian suffering, but this is the first I've seen that simultaneously gives permission to suffer without making you feel like it's your fault *and* gives permission to heal without turning to platitudes or feel-good theology. *Even If He Doesn't* takes the raw truth of suffering and mixes it with a gentle invitation to lean on the one who is with us through it all. And it's done with a bit of humor and levity that can only come from a life marked by joy and hope in the midst of deep sorrows.

CODY JAMES VERMILLION, Cofounder of Uncommon [good] Church, San Diego

In a humorous tearjerker, Kristen courageously reveals her experience through trauma, giving the reader a firsthand look at what it's like to have every certainty ripped from your suffering hands until all you're left with is a relationship with a God who is glad to be with you no matter what. Using her own story to expose harmful, distorted beliefs within Christian culture, Kristen creates space for the reader to find grace, peace, and joy in their journey.

TONI M. DANIELS, Operations director of LK10, coauthor of *Relational Revolution*, and podcast host of *Joy Fueled and Jesus Led*

It can be difficult to put words around suffering, loss, and grief. Kristen takes her story, woven beautifully with Scripture, and walks alongside the reader through their own feelings. I am very thankful for the grace and love that jump off the pages of this journey. Everyone deals with the pain of suffering differently— I'm thankful for Kristen's ability to help articulate a practical theology around a topic the church often struggles to explore.

TONY MILTENBERGER, Pastor and host of the *Reclamation Podcast*

Few are brave enough to address the topic of suffering because to believe in Jesus and suffer, too, can sometimes be a hard reality to accept. In this book, it feels like Kristen is holding our hand as she walks us through suffering and the sacred way to be in it while still hoping and believing in God. Every day, we are surrounded by suffering in this world, whether we see it or experience it—this book is for such a time as yesterday, today, and tomorrow.

PRICELIS PERREAUX-DOMINGUEZ, MSW, MS ED., Writer and founder of Full Collective

Kristen's words help us feel included—that our pain can be shared and understood. By the end of this book, God will feel closer and more real, and you will give yourself more love and compassion.

LEE ANN MILLER, TV personality

This book is a gift for those of us caught between hope in a God of love and the brutality of our own experience. Kristen LaValley courageously, transparently, invites us into her own journeys through this crucible. On the way, she brings fresh light, hope, and courage for our own roads ahead.

DR. KENT SMITH, Author, professor, and cofounder of the LK10 Network

The body is desperate for an honest expression of what it means to suffer while also walking with Jesus. In the wake of church hurt, loss, grief, and pain, Kristen offers a profound and earnest gift of words to believers everywhere and in any season of life. She wrestles well with the uncomfortable realities of loving Christ while living in the now and not yet.

BRENNA BLAIN, Contemporary theologian, author, and Bible teacher

In *Even If He Doesn't*, Kristen LaValley opens the door into her darkest moments with such honesty and straightforwardness that we can't help but feel less afraid to face our own valleys. Kristen writes with the voice of a friend—the kind who isn't afraid of your angst but also won't ever stop believing how beloved you are by God. This book felt like a balm to me personally, and I pray it offers the same to you. This is such a warm and welcoming book for all of us who can't unsee our own wounds.

K. J. RAMSEY, Therapist and author of *The Book of Common Courage* and *The Lord Is My Courage*

Even If He Doesn't

TYNDALE
MOMENTUM®

A Tyndale nonfiction imprint

EVEN IF HE
DOESN'T

What We Believe about God When Life Doesn't Make Sense

Kristen LaValley

Visit Tyndale online at tyndale.com.

Visit Tyndale Momentum online at tyndalemomentum.com.

Visit the author online at kristenlavalley.com.

Tyndale, Tyndale's quill logo, *Tyndale Momentum*, and the Tyndale Momentum logo are registered trademarks of Tyndale House Ministries. Tyndale Momentum is a nonfiction imprint of Tyndale House Publishers, Carol Stream, Illinois.

Even If He Doesn't: What We Believe about God When Life Doesn't Make Sense

Designed by Eva M. Winters

Edited by Stephanie Rische

The author is represented by Alive Literary Agency, www.aliveliterary.com.

For information about special discounts for bulk purchases, please contact Tyndale House Publishers at csresponse@tyndale.com, or call 1-855-277-9400.

Library of Congress Cataloging-in-Publication Data

A catalog record for this book is available from the Library of Congress.

ISBN 978-1-4964-7852-8

Printed in the United States of America

30	29	28	27	26	25	24
7	6	5	4	3	2	1

For Max.
Even though he didn't,
we know that one day he will.
We'll see you soon.

Contents

Author's Note

THROUGHOUT THE PROCESS OF WRITING, an important question has come up: "What gives me the right to write this book?" The pages you're about to read are about how crisis can devastate our faith and how painful and beautiful the rebuilding can be. I've experienced so much heartache in my life, but my biggest "Even if he doesn't" ended with "But he did."

I've wrestled quite a bit with that. Do I have the authority to write a book about suffering when we received the miracle we asked for? Why would anyone listen to me? Do I have the right to speak to hearts that carry tragedy I've never known?

The truth is, I don't. Our griefs are uniquely our own. Our suffering may be recognizable to others, but it's only intimately familiar to ourselves. When a mother and father lose a child, each of them experiences that grief in different ways. When a woman loses a husband, his mother loses a son. They both feel the loss, but the relationship to the grief is as different as their relationship to the person.

I can't speak to any individual suffering, even the kinds of suffering that look similar to my own. I can only speak to what I've learned from my own heartache.

In her book *Suffering Is Never for Nothing*, Elisabeth Elliot says, "Suffering is a mystery that none of us is really capable of plumbing. And it's a mystery about which I'm sure everyone at some time or other has asked why."[1] On these pages, I certainly don't claim to plumb the depths of every person's pain. If anyone were capable of writing an exhaustive study of the nuance and complexity of suffering, surely it would have already been written.

Instead, all I can do is offer my experiences and reflections. When we share our stories with each other and reflect on what we've learned through our pain, we're still only reflecting fragments that make up a larger theological and spiritual mystery. We can only know in part—this is my part. I haven't suffered in the same way or with the same intensity as others. I'm just familiar with its sting.

When we compare our suffering to someone else's, we're simply trying to make sense of what we're going through. In our attempt to understand a pain that is unfathomable and inexplicable, we measure our experience against what someone else is going through or has gone through. The result of that comparison is always the discrediting of pain.

If you compare your pain to someone else's and find yours to be greater, you diminish their suffering. If you compare your pain and find theirs to be greater, you diminish your own. And who can really scale the weight of suffering? I certainly can't.

What I do know is that most of us will experience suffering of some kind at some point in our lives. Your crisis may be considered significant by the standards of our culture (such as the loss of a child, the death of a spouse, a chronic disease, or a fatal diagnosis), or it may be something that the world considers "minor" but breaks your heart all the same.

No matter the width and depth of your pain, in this book you'll find the threads of faith both through answered prayers and in the middle of what felt like spiritual abandonment. Maybe my pain will be familiar to you; maybe it won't. Either way, hope and hard things are on the pages ahead of you. I hope you find yourself in them too.

Foreword

I AGREED TO WRITE Kristen's foreword for two reasons:

1. Kristen is a wordsmith unlike any I have run across in decades. This is the God-honest truth. She writes words like Steph Curry shoots threes. She writes paragraphs like Taylor writes bangers. It just seems so effortless.

2. I knew how important this book was going to be for so many people who have walked the hard road. Myself included . . .

But when I opened the box and the words *Even If He Doesn't* sat there, staring me in the face, in two seconds flat my mind accelerated toward all the still-empty shelves that were supposed to hold monuments to answered prayers I have prayed. I closed the box and said out loud, "Nope. Not today."

And I'm assuming that you may have experienced that same moment with this book. You may be reading these words months after you bought it because you just couldn't bring yourself to face some pain that you feel is purposeless. Or you may be ready to devour every page because you need some hope NOW. Well, let me tell you something: the fact that you are reading these words means that you are about to embark on a journey that won't exaggerate your pain but instead will literally be balm to your soul.

Pain has a way of moving us from carefree to cautious to calloused. From secure to suspect to cynical. That journey is a painful one, and the thought of ever getting back to a space where we are carefree and secure seems ultimately impossible. Well, I have some good news for you: this book is going to do just that. Don't stop reading until you hit the last word. Because if you are starting off reading this feeling like God has abandoned you because he didn't do something you begged of him, I have a feeling you will close this book, look up, and see that he has been sitting right next to you all along . . . even if he didn't.

Carlos Whittaker

Introduction

IF I HAD BEEN ASKED FIFTEEN YEARS AGO to write a book about hardship in the life of a believer, I would have been thrilled. With all the confidence of a recent Bible college graduate, I would have written that book emphatically. I would have huffed and puffed and passionately typed out all I knew about hardship, because my perspective hadn't yet been humbled from experiencing it. The main points of this hypothetical (*Thank you, Jesus*) book would probably be something like this:

Most hardship is caused by sin.

Some hardship isn't caused by sin, but we don't know why it happens—so just suck it up and trust God.

I come from a rich heritage of faith, and for most of my childhood and early adulthood, nothing really bad happened to any of us. I was convinced that my lack of childhood trauma and my family's protection from major heartache was because we were prayer warriors, faithful to the Lord, and free from sinful strongholds. So for me, faith was pretty formulaic: accept Jesus as your Lord and Savior + don't sin that much + tithe 10 percent = a happy life of minimal suffering.

If only it had stayed that simple.

In the last decade and a half, my simplistic view of suffering (and God's role in it) has crumbled and been rebuilt. But even with the pain I've experienced and now carry with me, I wouldn't want to go back to the naivete I had before I discovered how difficult life could be. I was relatively pain-free, but my faith was simple. If something went wrong, I blamed myself. I believed my actions, my immaturity, my selfishness, or my sins were the cause of my problems—even things that were out of my control. In my mind, everything could be explained, and most pain was avoidable.

When your life experiences follow the formula you believe in, you have no reason to question it. The equation feels simple, and your life serves as the proof. What a brutal grace it is to experience something that proves the formula problematic. Whether it's our own pain or the pain of someone we love, the experience will bring us to believe one of two outcomes.

The first is that when we encounter some kind of pain that doesn't fit our faith equation, our thoughts about God and our faith in him are shaken, sometimes to the point of abandoning our faith. The math of a pain-free life doesn't add up, which leads to the logical (albeit incorrect) conclusion that everything else we believe is also false.

The second outcome of a formulaic understanding of suffering is that it blocks us from truly caring for those around us who are hurting. When we believe that even the most brutal crisis can be easily explained or that sin is always the catalyst for pain, we place the fault and responsibility solely on the person in crisis. How can we bear the burden of a brother and sister in Christ if we believe their pain is their own fault? Can we truly follow the command to love each other if the side effect of our theology is conditional compassion? Can we really bootstrap people into complete healing?

Spoiler alert: the answer is no.

The other outcome is that the breaking of our formulas will lead us to a better understanding of the love of God. When we engage with our pain instead of bypassing it, we allow ourselves the opportunity to know God in—and through—our great hurts. As we grow in our knowledge of God's love and character, we can engage with others' hurts with grace, compassion, and gentleness.

I have walked through trials with shaky faith, and I've walked through them with unwavering faith. I've been the recipient of compassion and gentleness, and I've been blamed and accused of causing my own heartache. Sometimes my pain was too complicated for others to touch. So people stayed out of it, afraid to misplace their compassion in case what had happened was my fault. Sometimes my pain was received with warmth—but from a distance. At times my grief felt like too much for people to cross the threshold. Other times the body of Christ stepped into the thick of it without questions, loving me in a way enabled by Christ. In those moments when I could barely put one foot in front of the other, they were my breath, my voice, and my strength.

Through the painful moments, the paradigm shifts, the shaking of my faith, and the rebuilding of it, I have found the goodness of the Father at every turn. Sometimes all I had to hold on to were the pieces of my faith that hadn't been shaken by my pain. When my brain was foggy and I could barely open my Bible or utter a word of prayer, I'd repeat to myself things I knew to be true: he is good, he is kind, he is faithful, he is for me. Those truths were tied to the character of God—aspects of who I believed him to be that didn't need theological clarification. His faithfulness in my life had confirmed those unchangeable attributes over and over again.

When I didn't have the time or bandwidth to think, to process, to decide what I believed about something, the roots of my faith were planted so deeply that my decisions were instinctive. I knew what my belief system would compel me to decide without having to retrace the steps of how I got to that belief.

It wasn't always that way, of course. We don't suddenly become assured of what we believe when crisis hits. And often, that assurance is just certainty that hasn't been tested. When we allow suffering to teach us, and when we interact with others' suffering with openness and empathy, our theological best guesses get tested and tried and then they either take root or are ripped out. The ones that take root become spiritual instincts that guide us when we need it most.

Crisis tends to hit us out of nowhere, and we don't often have the time or emotional fortitude to rethink what we believe about God. It's in those moments that our faith becomes active. We move in step with what we already believe to be true about our Father, for better or for worse. We'll react differently to a situation if we believe God is good, kind, active, and faithful or if we believe he is distant, uncaring, and vengeful.

The way we were taught to pray, what we were taught to believe about suffering and the sovereignty of God, and how our community displays care for the hurting will shape the way we respond to trials. If we believe that suffering is always a consequence of sin, the blame we heap on ourselves will become self-hatred, which dishonors the image of God in us. If we've learned to pray only as a way to receive something from God, we'll feel like he has abandoned us when he doesn't answer. If the faith communities we're part of respond to pain with judgment and reservation, we'll never learn how to respond to others' suffering with compassion, grace, and generosity. But when we view suffering as something that we will all have to endure at some point, regardless of how good of a Christian we might be, and when we believe that God is present with us in it, we'll be able to get a clearer picture of who God is and who we are.

I grew up in a Christian family, surrounded by pastors and missionaries. My dad is a pastor, as was his dad and my mom's dad and most of their siblings—all in the same denomination. I went to Bible college in that denomination, so the messages about suffering I absorbed as a child were validated and doubled down on in my formal education.

My family was mostly suffering adjacent, observing the hardships of the people in our churches but never experiencing much loss firsthand. The message I observed and internalized was that there was always a reason someone was suffering. It was a consequence of something they'd done or a trial the Lord had given them to grow their faith. When hardship did come into our family, the solution was simple: just trust Jesus; don't ask why. I thought I needed faith the size of a mountain to endure whatever pain life (or God) brought my way.

Since then, I've walked through devastating spiritual wounds. I've grieved the loss of loved ones. I've suffered a violent miscarriage, witnessed a murder, and experienced the trauma of a high-risk twin pregnancy, an extended hospitalization, a premature delivery, and my babies' two-month stay in the NICU. I am more familiar than I'd like to be with pain and loss. But it would be foolish to consider myself an expert on suffering. I'm not. I simply have suffered. I don't know your story, but I think that if you picked up this book, you've probably had your share of pain too.

For the first couple of decades of my life, all I knew about pain was from observing it in others and studying it in books. But all the book knowledge, research, and theology in the world can't do for our hearts what crisis can. Heartbreak has a way of softening the edges in us that need to be softened while sharpening the ones that need sharpened. Our response to suffering can increase our capacity for hardship while deepening our empathy for those in pain.

Sometimes trials will surprise us in the most beautiful and complex ways. In the midst of the darkest pain, we may find flowers blooming in unexpected places. Like wildflowers growing in all the wrong spots, our faith will become more like a meadow and less like a math problem. Stories we've read in God's Word a hundred times will come alive in new ways. We'll find new friendships and connections that never would have grown without the pain that waters the soil of relationships.

At some point, most of us will experience the kind of unspeakable pain that shakes the foundations of everything we believe. When you find yourself walking through something so painful you can barely string together a coherent thought, I want you to have anchors to cling to, the comfort of the Spirit, a community of believers to hold up your arms, the peace of God, and the light of Christ to illuminate the fog that heartache brings. Maybe your faith needs a good shaking, as mine did. Maybe not. But in order to endure suffering with hope and strength, we need to take an honest look at what we believe about who God is and his relationship to our suffering. It's only then that we can sort the distorted truths from the real ones.

God meets us in the midst of all our days, and the painful ones are no exception. On the pages ahead, we'll learn how to hold on to faith when God doesn't answer the way we want him to and when it feels like he's not answering at all. You'll be invited to experience the God who is with you in your heartache, in your hardship, and in the complex pain in your life.

I won't promise too much, because there are no easy answers to pain.* While this isn't an exhaustive study on the theology of suffering, my hope is that reading this book will feel like having coffee with a friend who has walked a few steps ahead of you. By the time our cups are empty, we'll have unraveled some misconceptions about suffering, earned some hard-won wisdom, and wrapped ourselves up in a warm blanket of comfort for our spirits.

---

*I can, however, assure you that this is a much better read than whatever book I would have written fifteen years ago. There is no greater peace in my life than the knowledge that no one let me write a book in my early twenties.

1

When Your Image of God Shatters

How can I write you

to tell you that I'm angry

when I've been given the wrong address

and I don't even know your real name?

MADELEINE L'ENGLE

DURING ONE OF THE MOST PAINFUL seasons of my life, I was late-night scrolling one of these social media apps I pretend to hate. I was halfway through my pregnancy with identical twin girls, and my husband, Zach, and I had just found out they were not likely to survive.

As I scrolled aimlessly through my feed, trying to distract my mind and give myself something—*anything*—to think about other than the roaring sounds of grief and uncertainty, my finger stopped at an aesthetically designed quote. It was from one of the biggest, most influential churches of our time. It read, "Don't let your circumstances change the way you view God."

My nana always warned me that if I rolled my eyes, they'd get stuck, and now I know for sure that's not true because if it were, they definitely would have gotten themselves stuck that time. *Easy for you to say, Skinny Jeans,* I thought. Not that I knew whether he was wearing skinny jeans when he said it. Or that it was a *he* who said it. Or if it was easy for him to say. Or what circumstances Probably Wearing Skinny Jeans endured to come to the conclusion that we shouldn't allow our circumstances to change our view of God. I took a screenshot of the quote and sent it to my husband, adding, "Sometimes they do tho."

At the point of that late-night doomscrolling session, I was tired, emotionally exhausted in a way I'd never known before. I was completely uninterested in Christian platitudes and theological gotchas meant to jolt me into "correct" thinking. They might make you think, *Mmm, yeah, that's good.* You like it, you share it, and then you go on with your day. But in that moment, I didn't have an appetite for theological snacks.

I'd been through difficult things before. I'd experienced firsthand what it's like to have my image of God shatter into a million pieces because of circumstances that were out of my control. While I was hurting because of what happened to us, I was also trying to hold on to any shred of belief in a God who was suddenly not the God I thought I knew. These heartbreaks had changed how I viewed God and led me to a better understanding of him. Not before my heart bled out all of the images of him I'd created, but I eventually got there. It was a mercy for God to use my circumstances to change the way I viewed him. I hadn't truly known him until then.

But I'd never walked through anything like this before. I'd never been in a spot where every choice I made had the potential to write a death sentence.

There I found myself, in a crushing circumstance I hadn't asked for and hadn't caused, and this post was demanding that I hold on to how I viewed God. That wasn't really the issue for me. I knew who God was and believed in his goodness and faithfulness more than ever. But the only reason I'd gotten there was because my circumstances had demanded that I search and know God better.

So I did what I always do when a post on social media annoys me. I scrolled past it and allowed my mind to drift away from the reality I was facing. My babies were sick. They were, on paper, dying.

※

It was early March 2021. Zach and I had been together for fifteen years, married for twelve. Our kids were ten, eight, and seven. We were a few years out from a painful break with our church, where Zach had served as youth pastor, and we'd spent the last year traveling the country in an RV.

We'd been hoping to have another baby for almost two years at that point, so carrying *two* babies was an unexpected and welcome joy. We had no reason to believe that this ultrasound would be anything other than routine.

Wrong. So wrong. Maximum wrongness.

At the end of the scan, the maternal fetal medicine doctor came in and introduced herself and said, "I'm sorry to meet you like this."

I don't remember what she said after that. I'd read memoirs by people who have gone through something traumatic, and I'd never really thought about how they were able to recall so many details from the experience. That wasn't the case for me—my memories are spotty, fading in and out. I remember the doctor's face. I remember the silence of the tech beside her. I remember how cold my phone felt in my hands. I remember wrapping my arms around my body in an attempt to comfort myself. I remember the doctor reaching out and touching my knee. I remember the room spinning. I remember feeling like I wanted to rip off all my clothes and run away. But I don't remember the initial impact of the explosion.

My memory kicks in somewhere around the time of the doctor's crude drawing of my uterus. She sketched two stick-figure babies inside a circle and drew two squiggly lines from their bellies to represent their umbilical cords. She then connected those squiggly lines to an oval shape representing their single shared placenta.

The doctor explained that Baby B wasn't getting enough blood through her umbilical cord. She was small—too small. She was weak. She wasn't likely to survive to a viable gestational age. If she died, her death would send a surge of blood into the shared placenta, which would go straight to Baby A's heart. This would likely cause Baby A to die as well or, at the very least, to have a life-altering stroke. She would never lead a normal life.

"You do have options, though," the doctor told me.

She explained a procedure that would save Baby A by lasering the umbilical cord of Baby B. I didn't fully understand what she was saying until she took her pen and drew a large X through Baby B's squiggly umbilical cord, representing its detachment from the placenta.

"Oh my God!" I choked.

The doctor startled a bit, blinking her eyes a few times. "I know this is so difficult to hear," she said. I could tell she was trying to remain neutral and controlled.

"Are you recommending that I terminate one baby to save the other baby?"

She nodded sympathetically. "Yes, that's the option some mothers in your situation choose."

Oh my God. Oh my God. Oh my God.

The sobs that escaped my chest were guttural. "There has to be another way. There has to be another option. I want them both. Oh God, I want them both."

In one instant, I was thrown into the valley of the shadow of death, left to decide the fate of our daughters while holding on to the hope that God would make it all okay. Don't let my circumstances change the way I view God? *Why not?*

When crisis hits, it presents us with a choice. Will we stubbornly cling to what we've always believed, even when it no longer makes sense in our circumstances? Or will we respond to the crisis as an invitation to know him more? When we've decided we have God figured out, our firmly held beliefs become security blankets. We might even be convinced that it would be wrong or sinful to change our minds.

So instead of leaning into our pain and our questions, we turn away from them, cozy up with what we're confident is right, and deny ourselves the grace of knowing God *through* our pain, not just in spite of it. In pain, God becomes full, vibrant color.

The key difference between religion and faith is that while religion stands still and quiet, faith chases, pursues, and seeks. Faith moves us. We run after him with limps. We praise with no words. We sing with no song. We search for him in the dark, we reach out our hands to make contact, and we turn our heads toward him and whisper, "Are you still there?" Even when he doesn't whisper back, we continue to speak, to crawl, to try to find some shred of the God we still somehow, inexplicably, believe is there in the dark with us.

What I *hope* that quote I stumbled on that night was trying to express is that our experiences often tempt us to believe that God is something he isn't. That he's against us. That he's cruel. That he's a dad who leaves when we mess up. But maybe there's a better thing to say and teach about suffering: that we can allow our circumstances to reveal the truth of God's character and shake out everything that doesn't reflect who he is.

> In pain, God becomes full, vibrant color.

When we're in the middle of a reality we never dreamed would be ours, we don't have to hold on to our image of God so tightly that our fingers practically break. Instead, we can offer up this simple prayer: "God, use this to reveal to me who you are and break any false images I've made of you."

Clearly, I'm not a fan of theological quips that put the fault of a changed perspective on a person whose circumstances are crushing them. Suffering isn't always someone's "fault." Neither is a changed perspective. Changing your mind about something you were wrong about is a grace given to us by the Father, who can use our pain to show us who he really is.

Faith moves us. We run after him with limps.

When you're at the bottom of a pit, and you're cold and hungry and tired, and it's dark, and someone yells out, "Hey! Are you bleeding? Can you hear me? Listen, I have to tell you something, and this is really gonna help you! Don't let this change your mind about God! Okay, bye!" what do you think your response will be? Do you think you'll reply with a hearty, "You know what? You're right! Gee, thanks for that, buddy!"

Yeah, I don't think so. Your response will most likely be a desperate grasp at anything you can hold on to before whisper-yelling back, "I'm trying. I'm trying. I want him to be who I believe him to be. I want him to be here with me."

And also . . . maybe throw down a rope?

The truth is that circumstances *can* change our minds about God—and that's not always a bad thing. But it's also not a fun thing. Once you're committed to the way you see things, it's hard to see the world any other way, even when presented with convincing evidence.

Let me tell you a story about Emily. I need you to read it like I wrote it. With narrowed eyes and a bit of snarled lip: *Emily.*

When I was in first grade, I went over to Emily's house for a playdate. Emily had a *playroom*. A whole room full of toys that were just hers. I'd never seen anything like it in my life. A room for toys? Where did her mom put her sewing machine? Where did her dad put his books? Where did they sleep? These were questions I never got answers to because that day was about playing with our dolls, and Emily wanted to braid their hair.

Not many people can pinpoint a moment in their childhood that changed the way they interacted with the world, but I can. This was it. I sat there in absolute shame as every other girl at the playdate braided her doll's hair . . . except me. I couldn't do it—I didn't know how.

I fumbled my fingers and twisted strands and said, "I did it!" But my classmates only laughed at me for being stupid. They didn't say that, but they kind of did, with their eyes.

When I got home from that playdate, I went straight to my dolls (they could all fit on my bed—I didn't have a whole room full of them) and sat there twisting and pulling and crying until I figured out how to do a beautiful three-strand braid. I would braid the hair to the very tip, unravel it, and do it again. Over and over and over again. On different sized dolls, in different places on the dolls' heads. Ponytails, pigtails—you name it, I braided it.

I would never, ever for the rest of my life be caught not knowing how to do something.

The next morning, I walked confidently into my classroom, head held high, fingers itching to prove my worth. I went straight to Emily and said, "I can do it! I can braid hair!"

She laughed. "No, you can't. You don't know how."

I was adamant. "No, really, I can do it! Watch!"

I had my friend with the longest hair sit down in front of me. As Emily watched, I braided the girl's hair from top to bottom.

I tied it off with a scrunchie and everything. I looked at Emily, eager for her approval.

But Emily, Professional Braider, crossed her arms. "You didn't do that."

I'm sorry, what?

Even our friends were like, "Girl, what?"

"Yes, I did," I said. "You just watched me do it!"

She looked me up and down. "No, you didn't." And then she walked away with all our friends.

Somehow Emily convinced our entire class to believe I didn't know how to braid even though they'd all just *watched me do it.*

But who gets the last braid now, *Emily?* Now the world knows that I can braid and you're the girl who gaslit an entire first-grade class!

The point of this story isn't to show you the childhood wounds that are still gaping in my life (obviously, I am fully healed from this one) but to show you that sometimes people refuse to change their minds even when the evidence is alarmingly stacked against their long-held beliefs. This isn't only true for the first-grade crowd; it also applies to things we've been taught about God that aren't actually true about him. Pride keeps a death grip on things that cost too much to let go of. Fear prevents us from asking tough questions that lead to a deeper understanding of God and his Word.

For the sake of intellectual honesty and spiritual sincerity, we have to be willing to change our minds sometimes. We need to take the risk of pursuing truth, even if it comes at the cost of changing our minds about things we were sure were right. Fear and pride only keep us from the presence of God. They keep us from knowing him and from diving into the fullness of Christ with our full selves.

✳

I have a big red tub full of all the things I've written down, dating from right around the time I learned to write. There are journals, poems, songs, letters, and notes scribbled onto airplane napkins. It's a history of my life, my thoughts, and my faith—a sort of coming-of-age story of a kid who grew up "saved."

These days, it serves as a memorial for the fragile fragments of my faith that shattered when crisis hit. I can follow the breadcrumbs of my life and mark these moments—from smaller events, like getting fired from a job I loved and breaking up with a guy I thought I'd marry to things that truly shook the earth under my feet.

Every Christian learns a theology of suffering. Most of us don't learn this in a classroom or by studying academic books; we sort of pick up an understanding over time. We hear messages from teachers, pastors, social media posts, or conversations with mentors and peers, and we internalize them without really stopping to think them through. We tend to absorb these beliefs experientially as we respond to suffering.

We share our theologies about suffering more in the way we respond to suffering than in the systematic teaching of it.

"Did you hear what happened to John?"

"Yes, I did. God must really be trying to teach him something."

We nod our heads, thankful we aren't the ones God is trying to teach, and we never really think through the implications of the conclusions we draw. It doesn't feel important until it's relevant to our own lives. Unfortunately, by the time suffering knocks on our door, it's too late to develop a more robust theology about it. Our beliefs are already there, informing how we feel, how we act, and how we engage with our pain.

Most of the time, we don't really know the strength of our

beliefs until they're tested. When what we believe to be true about God and what we experience have always been aligned, we don't have any reason to think we're wrong. The framework seems solid: A + B has always equaled C, so we must have it right.

But what happens when we experience something that directly challenges what we believe to be true?

When we're faced with something we never expected, we either try to make our experience fit our theology or try to make our theology fit our experience. We can choose to close our eyes and ears and scream, "La la la" and ignore the fire in our chest that burns from our feelings of abandonment and doubt. Uncertainty is scary territory for the theologically confident. We wouldn't doubt if we had enough faith, and if we don't have enough faith we'll fall into sin, and if we fall into sin were we ever really his at all? So instead, we pretend that the doubt isn't there. We tuck it away, lock it up, and throw away the key.

We grab our theology in one hand and our experience in the other. We slam them together, trying to force them to come together in a way that makes sense, even though they're repelling each other like opposing sides of magnets. But something has to give. This is when we need to take a look at what we're holding on to and drop the things that we shouldn't have had a tight grasp on in the first place.

I don't know what those unguaranteed absolutes are for you. Were you taught that if you pray hard enough, you'll get your miracle? That you only suffer when you have unconfessed sin? That if you have enough faith, the person you love will be healed? That your faith community will stand beside you perfectly in your suffering, knowing exactly when you need a hug or a casserole? That God will move in ways that are predictable and make sense in the here and now?

The reality is that some things are too heavy to carry in the same hands as your unwavering faith. It's hard to hold on when your hands are shaking, so you drop some things and steady yourself. If one of the things you drop is the comfort of a faith that's never been challenged, it frees your grasp to hold on to what you can be sure of: the presence of a good and faithful Creator.

When my own suffering tore me to shreds, there was no book, no Scripture, no sermon, no well-meaning words from a friend that could undo the unraveling that was happening in my life. Suffering has a way of forcing us to look directly at things we've been content to leave unquestioned in the past. When you feel like God hasn't fulfilled his end of your saved-to-Savior relationship, you feel betrayed. When you feel betrayed, trust is gone. When trust is gone, so is the relationship.

I needed to reexamine each piece of the framework of my faith if I was ever going to believe anything good about God again.

When we're standing exposed in the cold winds of suffering, it's easy to land in one of two places: *this is my fault* or *this is God's fault*.

If you've absorbed a theology that says suffering is always the result of sin, then when something bad happens, you go searching for sin that might not even be there. You blame yourself and beat yourself up until eventually you either resign yourself to a life of self-flogging or accept that your theology isn't as airtight as you thought.

I'm not sure what's worse: believing that God is punishing you for some unknown sin or believing that God is just that unkind. The most devastating of all conclusions to draw from suffering is that God has rejected you.

It's a lie, of course. It's the same lie that the enemy has been planting in human hearts since the beginning. Satan is convinced that with the right amount of pain, God's people will believe he is against them and they'll reject him. Imagine his audacity in telling God that if enough things were taken away from a man, he'd curse God to his face.*

The book of Job is about a man who lost everything. He trusted God, and his suffering wasn't the result of his sin. Yet God didn't spare his health or his home or his children or his livelihood. Job's entire story is a series of "even if he doesn't" events.

Just as he did with Job, the enemy tries to use the vulnerability of our pain to convince us that the most intrinsic piece of our faith—that God loves us—isn't true. When the enemy can manipulate our perspective so much that we doubt the love of God, our image of God becomes fractured.

The way we view God affects the way we see everything. It changes the way we interact with each other, the way we experience joy, and the way we experience pain. If we believe that God's love is unreliable or transactional, then the responsibility of his affection relies on us. We think we have to work hard to keep his gaze fixed on us. *Don't mess up, or he'll turn away!* But that isn't true.

God loves you. Full stop. No qualifiers. No "Yeah, but . . ." He loves you. Even when you sin. "While we were still sinners, Christ died for us."†

Yes, sin has consequences. In some cases, we can look at the destruction in our lives and say, "Oh, look, if it isn't the consequences of my own actions." Hebrews 12 shows us that sometimes God does allow suffering to teach us and discipline us. Of course, sin and selfishness can bring significant measures of pain and suffering into our lives. But God is not standing there waiting for us to sin, dangling his love like a carrot for us to chase. Even when we sin, he doesn't remove his love from us.

---

*Job 1:11
† Romans 5:8

Suffering can be a result of sin, whether as the natural conse-quence of an individual sin or because of the universal existence of sin in the world. But sometimes bad things happen and it's no one's fault. Suffering, in itself, is not a sign that you have hidden sin God is punishing you for. Theology like that is incomplete because it fails to account for the work of the Cross, where Christ took the punishment of sin and death *for* us.

For argument's sake, let's take the absolute worst-case sce-nario. Let's say you're a filthy, wicked sinner and God has allowed suffering in your life as a direct punishment for your sinful choices. Even if that's true, God still has not rejected you. He still loves you. He's still for you. The most important thing to remember about God is that he is redemptive, not vindictive. All he does, he does in love—to draw us to himself, not push us away from him.

The story of God and his people is one of failure (on our part) and perpetual second chances (on his part). In every moment of our lives on earth, we are given the opportunity for redemption and reconciliation. So if there's nothing we can do to separate ourselves from the love of God,* that means we are loved by him even in our sin, even in the consequences.

Whether your suffering is a natural suffering, independent of sin, or if it's suffering brought on by sin (yours or someone else's), he is still drawing near to you and drawing you to himself. He has not turned his face from you. You aren't hidden from him, even if you're in sin.

When I was in college, I was diagnosed with ovarian cysts. With my future husband (who was "just a friend" at the time) by my

---

* *Romans 8:39*

side, the doctor told me I would likely never have children. I was stunned. Zach and I barely spoke on the drive back to campus while I shed a few silent tears from the passenger seat.

As I processed the diagnosis later with a group of friends, I expressed that I felt like this diagnosis and "the closing of my womb" (because in Bible college, you talk like that) was because of my sin. My friends were quick to shut down that idea and remind me that God is merciful and kind.

As I struggled with what my life would look like moving forward, I was comforted by another incorrect simplification of suffering: that suffering is proof we're directly in the middle of God's will for our lives.

While it's true that God can use our suffering to form our character and make us more like him, simply belonging to him doesn't put a target on our backs for suffering. The idea that God *wants* us to suffer (for any reason) stands in direct contradiction to the life, testimony, and work of Christ. Jesus came to take our suffering on himself, not to have us prove something by our own suffering.

This misconception is the opposite of "I'm suffering because of my sin," but in some ways it's worse because it says, "I'm suffering because God approves of me." If you follow this train of thought logically, this would mean that if you have peace, if you have no suffering, you're far from God. This theology implies that if we're in God's will, we'll suffer.

Suffering is a pretty terrible litmus test for whether we're doing the right things. I know people who deeply love the Lord who have not walked through extreme suffering. I know people who do not know the Lord who have experienced unspeakable tragedy. If the equation doesn't work every time, the equation is wrong. The presence or absence of suffering is not a cheat code to determine whether we're in the will of God.

Instead of judging your heart by your suffering, judge it by the

Spirit. Instead of looking at your suffering as some sort of inevitability to serving Christ well, look at your suffering through the lens of someone who has a Savior. We will all experience some level of suffering in our lives, and we would do well to remember that we're not victims of our suffering. Jesus didn't just defeat sin and death on the cross; he also defeated the effects of sin and death. You may not escape suffering, and Scripture tells us as much. But don't get comfortable in it, and don't be proud of it either, waving it around as if it's some kind of badge of honor.

One day, while we were in the thick of navigating our daughters' diagnosis, I was listening to a song with lyrics that went something like "I want you to put me in the fire, Jesus. Try me by fire!" I sat there in my car, shaking my head, talking out loud to whoever was singing: "Are you sure about that? Do you actually want that?" I pictured all the tragedy and loss I'd walked through, and the thought that someone would pray for that was wild to me. No amount of romanticizing suffering would make me want to sing those lyrics. *I'm done, Lord! I want to be tried by fuzzy blankets and cups of tea!*

As long as you're breathing, never stop asking for healing. Never stop praying for peace. Never stop believing for redemption. Jesus is with you in your suffering. The promise is not that you won't suffer but that he is with you in your suffering, offering peace and hope, and leading you to calmer waters.

Instead of saying, "My suffering is proof that I'm in the will of God," we can say, "Jesus came to bear the weight of our suffering. His death and resurrection give me hope that I won't be stuck in this unrelenting pain. He is a God of redemption, and he always offers a way out."

When we reframe our understanding of suffering in a more truthful, tangible way, we'll have something with roots to hold on to when life turns us completely upside down.

When you're in pain, you don't want to depend on words God has already spoken; you want something new! When he's been quiet for a while, we start to believe he's distant. But that's never true—he's always speaking, always moving, always drawing his people to his heart. We won't always recognize it and it won't always come the way we expect it to, but that doesn't mean God has removed himself from us.

When I look back at the years when I felt he wasn't around, I can clearly see how he was actively working on my behalf. On the same days I wrote things in my journal like "Do you even care about us anymore?" details were being lined up in the perfect way so they would happen at the perfect time. I couldn't see it yet, so it was hard to believe it. It's only when the fog of suffering lifts that we can recognize how God was intervening.

Exodus 3:7 captures these words from the Lord to his people, who were suffering under the oppressive rule of Pharaoh in Egypt: "I have indeed seen the misery of my people in Egypt. I have heard them crying out because of their slave drivers, and I am concerned about their suffering." Even if you don't feel God or see him or hear him in the way you were taught to expect, he is the God who sees and the God who is concerned.

Grief has a way of consuming our thoughts. We start to draw conclusions like *I haven't heard from God, so either he isn't real or he doesn't care.* Write this down to remind you what is true: "God is present and active in my life, but he might not always speak the way I expect." When God called Elijah to the mountain so he could speak to him, there was a wind that shattered the cliffs, but God wasn't in the wind. Then there was an earthquake, but he wasn't in that either. After the earthquake, there was a fire, but

God wasn't in the fire. God was in what came last: a whisper.[*] Even in the middle of the darkest night, your heart—even if just a fragment of it—can trust that he is actively present in your life.

The reality is, we want our pain to count for something. We can't imagine a world in which a good and kind Creator would let us suffer for nothing. So we take our pain and dissect it and dig through the layers of dirt to try to extract some sort of design from it. *Maybe he's trying to teach me patience. Maybe he's trying to teach me grace. Maybe he's allowing me to go through this so I can teach someone else.* We search endlessly for meaning, because how could a good God waste our pain?

But not everything that happens in our lives is supposed to be some grand heavenly lesson. It's true that our suffering is never wasted. Our pain isn't purposeless. But we may never know why while we're here on earth. In fact, I think it's safe to assume we likely won't be given explanations for our pain. When we're obsessed with finding the purpose for everything, we're seeking comfort in the purpose rather than the comfort of Christ.

But even if we don't know the reasons, we can know the Father. Instead of saying, "God is trying to teach me something—I have to figure out what it is so I can learn my lesson and end my suffering," we can say, "I don't know whether I'm supposed to be learning something here. I'll stay open to the teaching of the Holy Spirit and trust the Lord to bring peace and healing, regardless of whether I have something to learn."

> When we're obsessed with finding the purpose for everything, we're seeking comfort in the purpose rather than the comfort of Christ.

When we stop trying to squeeze purpose from our pain, we can rest in the peace of God. His peace—the peace that "transcends

---

[*] *1 Kings 19:11-12*

all understanding"—will hold our hearts perfectly when we don't understand.*

The people of God have been asking him "Why?" since the beginning of creation, and they are rarely given an answer. But he gives us his peace. And that is enough.

Suffering has every right to shake your confidence, but it doesn't have to destroy your faith. So let your paradigms shake a little and see what shakes out. You might find yourself left with a much truer and more beautiful understanding of grace, the work of the Cross, and the presence of God in your suffering.

When I sat in that cold hospital room, holding the sudden weight of a crisis pregnancy, I had already experienced the kind of earthquakes that shake your faith to its roots. I'd already been shaken, and I'd already rebuilt from the fragments of faith that were left. Those fragments became the foundation for a belief system that kept me grounded when my entire world was crumbling around me.

I didn't know what was going to happen with our daughters. I didn't know if they were going to live or die. But I knew that God loved me. And I knew that he was faithful, even though it might have looked like he'd abandoned us. While I didn't understand why he was allowing my pregnancy to be clouded by heartbreak, I knew that he was with us and that he would stay with us until the end, no matter what that ending might be.

---

*Philippians 4:7

THE DISTORTION:
Suffering can always be explained.

❁

THE SHIFT:
I might not know the reason I'm suffering,
but I know God is present with me in it.

2

What Crisis Reveals

God has not been trying an experiment on my faith or love in order to find out their quality. He knew it already. It was I who didn't. In this trial He makes us occupy the dock, the witness box, and the bench all at once. He always knew that my temple was a house of cards. His only way of making me realize the fact was to knock it down.

C. S. LEWIS

OUR FAMILY OF FIVE HAD SPENT the last three years rebuilding our lives and healing from a painful split from our church. After we left the church, we'd decided to plant our feet firmly on the ground and build a life outside of career ministry, for the first time ever.

At the beginning of 2020, we were healthy, happy, and itching for a change of scenery and a bit of adventure. So with three elementary school aged kids, we decided to sell just about everything we owned, end the lease on our home in Massachusetts, and purchase a thirty-two-foot trailer. Our lease ended March 7, 2020.

We were days away from starting our trip when the whole world shut down. With no place to call home, no real beds to sleep on, not a single chair to sit in, no campgrounds to park in, and in a climate that was too cold for our trailer to handle, we drove south and parked in our friends' driveway in Florida.

We rode the wave of the early part of the quarantine clustered together. Six weeks later, we set off. We'd always planned to spend a year on the road, but the shutdowns, restrictions, protests, and riots forced us to hold our plans with open hands. We traveled cautiously, visited a few friends, saw a few national parks, and made memories with our kids.

After seven months on the road, I took a pregnancy test at a Target in Phoenix and found out that our travel plans would be changing in all the best ways.

The pregnancy was rough from the start. I began throwing up almost immediately. I struggled to walk even short distances because I got tired and sick so easily. Most days I could barely get out of bed.

Zach would take the kids on little adventures during the day. Sometimes I'd hear them making fires and playing silly games outside the trailer, and I'd lie in my bed, crying and scrolling aimlessly on my phone, wishing I could join them. Every now and then I'd try to put my feet on the ground and do something fun, only to immediately regret the decision and make everyone else miserable in the process.

One night a few months into the pregnancy, I was so sick I couldn't even keep water down. In an act of desperation, my sweet husband drove to a friend's house in the middle of the night to retrieve her seven-year expired anti-nausea meds. They worked long enough for me to put something in my stomach, but it wasn't long before the cycle started again.

I relieved myself of my meals in some pretty creative places, and I don't know if you've ever slept in a travel trailer or driven long distances in a giant pickup truck pulling a travel trailer, but just imagine getting on a roller coaster with a stomach bug, and you'll have a pretty good idea of what it was like.

I was miserable and losing weight rapidly. Zach and I decided to make one more trip to Florida so I could ride out the worst of my pregnancy misery there. Florida was an easy place for us to be. When you're sick, you don't want to go on an adventure; you want to be somewhere familiar. That's what Florida was for us.

We parked at an RV park a few minutes from several family members. At the time, it felt like we were just putting one foot in front of the other. But looking back, we can see it wasn't just a practical decision; it was the Lord's leading that brought us to Florida.

I was seeing a midwife through my ob-gyn's practice, and we'd decided I didn't need to go in until my twenty-week anatomy scan. I'd had pretty textbook pregnancies in the past, with no complications and quick, natural births. All my appointments were done virtually, and honestly, I loved it.

I'd already had three kids, and I knew what to watch out for, when to worry, and when not to worry. I was confident that I knew my body and could trust it. Neither I nor my midwife had any reason to be concerned that this pregnancy would be any different from the others. Aside from the fact that I was approaching "geriatric" status at the ripe old age of thirty-four, there were no red flags or concerns.

After my first virtual call with the midwife, Zach and I joked that I could probably do her job at this point. "I could pop this baby out right here with no help, and we could pack up and drive to another spot the next day. No problem!"

Ah, the arrogance of ignorance.

With our other pregnancies, we'd waited until birth or until the midpregnancy scan to find out the gender of the baby. But this time we were too excited to wait. Our kids were nine, seven, and five by now, and they were all in with this pregnancy. They were eager to find out if they were getting a baby brother or a baby sister.

Zach had never missed a doctor's appointment or ultrasound with any of our other kids. But now we were in a pandemic that would prevent him from attending any of the milestone medical visits with me. It broke my heart that he'd be missing out on so much.

So when we found out there were ultrasound businesses that existed for the sole purpose of letting you find out the gender of your baby—and that your family and friends could join you—we jumped at the chance.

I was only fourteen weeks along, so I knew it wasn't guaranteed that we'd be able to learn the baby's gender. But with how sick I had been, I had a suspicion it was twins, and the not knowing was killing me. I thought, *Even if we aren't able to find out the gender, at least it'll put my mind at ease when they confirm there's only one baby.* Oh, how God laughs.

Our trailer was parked a few miles from my cousin Danielle's house. Danielle has the same proclivity toward stirring pots that I have toward impulsivity—so when she texted me the location of the ultrasound facility and asked me if I was interested, we were in the car in less than ten minutes.

If we hadn't been in Florida, close enough for Danielle to get the idea and close enough for us to act on this impulse together, we would have waited until my scheduled ultrasound. If we'd waited, I would have found out that we were having twins *and* that they were in crisis at the same time—alone, hundreds of miles away from my husband and kids. Instead, we found out together we were having two babies—a moment that was nothing but joy and excitement, separated from fear and crisis.

We had no idea how many doctor's appointments there would end up being or how difficult they would be. We didn't know about the hospital bathroom I would cry in and try to gather myself together in before walking to the car, where Zach and the kids were waiting. We didn't know how alone I would be in this pregnancy. In retrospect, I know that this silly little gender reveal scan was something that God had aligned for us. It was the last normal thing in a pregnancy that would be full of fear, chaos, and the unknown.

In the parking lot of the shopping plaza before the scan, Danielle took out her phone to document everyone's gender guesses. Then she giggled and said, "How *many* do you think you're having?"

Pot stirrer, remember? I rolled my eyes.

Our oldest said a confident, "One."

Our youngest said the same.

Then our middle son shouted, "Two!"

Danielle panned the camera to me. "You'd better all say *one*," I said.

The idea of two babies was way too wild. I'd tried to convince myself that my sneaking suspicions were just my flair for theatrics and a desire to add a little spice to my life. There was no way I was having two babies.

A few minutes later, we were all huddled together in the back room of the ultrasound business. My kids squeezed in with my husband, Danielle sat on the couches next to me, and we watched as the ultrasound lit up on the giant screen.

Danielle saw it right away. "Are there *two*?" she asked.

The ultrasound tech dragged the wand across my belly and kind of giggled a yes.

I didn't think she was being serious—I thought maybe she'd misunderstood what Danielle was asking. Or maybe she was being sarcastic. I figured she had people making twin jokes all the time.

She's just being nice, I thought. Listen, there are a lot of things I can do, but believing what's right in front of my face is not one of them.

As the tech adjusted the image, I narrowed my eyes at the screen. *Hang on*, I thought. *Does that baby have two heads?* Barely had the thought formed in my mind when the ultrasound tech said, quite matter-of-factly, as if she weren't about to turn my entire world upside down, "There's A and B."

Record scratch.

"Wait," I said. "Are you saying there are two babies?"

She whipped her head toward me, eyes wide with shock. "YES! You didn't know?"

NO, I DIDN'T KNOW.

Danielle screamed. The kids started running in circles.

Zach, in total denial, kept saying, "Nuh-uh. You're joking. You're a jokester. I need receipts. I need receipts."

I pulled my mask off my face so my jaw could hang open as far as possible.

Danielle ran over to me and shook my arm. "Why aren't you saying anything? We need to call your mom!"

As chaos ensued around me, the ultrasound tech continued the scan. Then she turned to me and said, "You really didn't know?"

"No," I told her, wiping my tears. Then I took a breath. "We lost a baby last year."

Why did I tell her that? I don't know. I think I just needed someone to hear it. I needed to put it out in the air—the acknowledgment of what we'd lost in the excitement of the gift we were being given. Tears fell down my cheeks faster than I could stop them.

She whispered, "Don't make me cry at work."

We both felt the weight of what was happening. I'd lost a baby. And now I had two.

Whatever our circumstances reveal to us about our beliefs, we have to decide what to do with the revelation. We can ignore the inconsistencies and incompleteness of what we've assumed to be true and deflect from them with trite Christian words. Or we can engage with the space between what we believe and what we're living out.

We don't have to be afraid of what heartache will reveal in us. It might show us how far we've come and how strong our beliefs are. It might expose theology that's incorrect and harmful. No matter what is revealed, it's ultimately good, because it presents an opportunity to enrich our faith. When we reevaluate our faith, it isn't a sign of weakness or spiritual immaturity. It's an opportunity to grow.

In the midst of your crisis, you may find yourself thinking, *But look at what I've done for the Kingdom! I've been good, I've been righteous, I've tithed, I've given faithfully. How can this be happening to me?* If so, your theology has without a doubt been shaped by the gospel that teaches that the love and favor of God are transactional: *If I do this, God will do that.* This way of thinking easily (and subtly) turns into *If I do this, God owes me that.*

Suffering reveals the prosperity gospel in us. When God doesn't hold up his end of the bargain even though we held ours up, we get angry. We expect a return on our investment. And when we suffer anyway, we believe God has betrayed our contract. But that's not faith, that's not a relationship; that's a transaction. When we embrace this way of thinking (often unintentionally), we reject the sovereignty of God and try to put some element of control into our own hands.

There's a huge difference between God promising something to us and God owing us something. It's the difference between faith and entitlement. When we believe God owes us, we think we're guaranteed wealth, health, and security simply because we checked off the boxes needed to get the return from our Creator. But oh, does

> *Crisis reveals what we have faith in.*

our world implode when we check all the boxes and don't get the blessing.

Crisis reveals what we have faith in. Do we have faith in God indiscriminately? Not based on what he does, what he has done, or what we think he's going to do but just for who he is? Do we believe that he is good unconditionally, even when things don't go our way? Are we willing to let go of our death grasp on the things we think will give us peace and security, and put our faith in God instead? Do we believe that he is for us, he is with us, and he cares for us without requiring us to do something to deserve it or earn it? Do we have more faith in our theology being right than in God being good? Is God still good even if our doctrines are wrong?

When our image of God is dependent on things going the way we believe they should, our image of him is centered on us, not on him. But true faith isn't believing God is good just because we have proof of it. Faith is believing that he's good even when we don't have proof.

People change their theology all the time. Churches split, theses get nailed to walls, and people do deep dives to see how the Bible lines up with (or doesn't line up with) what they've been taught. Does any of that change who God is? Of course not! God's character is constant and steady. He doesn't change. He doesn't move. He isn't shaped by our beliefs about him. He's outside our understanding! If our theology proves to be wrong, God is still God. Crisis exposes to us how much of our faith is in our *understanding* of God and how much of it is actually in God himself.

> *True faith isn't believing God is good just because we have proof of it. Faith is believing that he's good even when we don't have proof.*

Nothing tests the integrity of our beliefs like finding ourselves in a situation we never thought we'd be in. It's easy to look at someone else walking through something difficult and confidently assert how we'd handle it and what decisions we'd make. But when the shoes are on our own feet, it's not as easy as it looks. Crisis exposes whether our beliefs about God have shaped our character into something that reflects Christ.

Crisis exposes to us how much of our faith is in our understanding of God and how much of it is actually in God himself.

Who are you when you have nothing left to lose or gain? Suffering has a way of showing us how important we think we are. Pride is put on display in ways we can't predict or prevent. But we get a choice—a character-shaping choice. Crisis gives us the chance to repent of beliefs we've held that caused us to judge or withhold compassion from others. Will we accept this opportunity? Or will we double down and find ways to excuse ourselves from the conclusions we've made about others' faith and integrity?

Character is easy to fake when it isn't tested. But when the fire comes, it will burn off all our pretense and expose who we really are. This is a good thing. A beautiful thing, even.

Christians often offer warnings about the dangers of doubt. There's a fear that if we ask too many questions, those questions will lead us into some kind of spiritual wilderness. But even the Bible tells stories of men and women of faith who didn't hold back from asking God tough questions. Abraham questioned God's justice, asking, "Won't the Judge of the whole earth do what is just?"[*] David asked God why he hid "in times of trouble."[†] Moses asked God why he sent him at all when it had only caused more trouble for God's people.[‡] Even Jesus asked his Father, "Why have you forsaken me?"[§]

---

[*] *Genesis 18:25,* CSB
[†] *Psalm 10:1*
[‡] *Exodus 5:22*
[§] *Matthew 27:46*

Being afraid to confront our fears keeps us standing still when God is inviting us to step closer. We might have to trudge through some weeds, but we'll eventually find the meadow. And the things that grow past our hurts and shattered faith frameworks are a little wild and a lot good.

It's easy to walk through life unaware of how our theology is harming us or other people. So when we're given the opportunity to engage with our beliefs and gain a more intimate understanding of who God is, it's not a punishment; it's a grace.

Zach was in Florida with our kids, and I'd just flown to Massachusetts for what was supposed to be our standard mid-pregnancy anatomy scan.

It was anything but that.

The scan lasted more than two hours. I chitchatted a bit with the tech, but it was mostly quiet. I watched as the images of my babies appeared on the screen, showing all their tiny parts. Twenty fingers, twenty toes, two heartbeats, four legs, four arms—the whole thing blew my mind. Never before had I felt so much marvel at an ultrasound. And never before had I realized how many things have to go right for a baby to be born healthy.

I felt the girls move around and watched them squirm when the ultrasound wand pressed against their backs and tummies. My cheeks hurt from how much I was grinning. Grateful doesn't begin to describe what it felt like to see two fully formed, fully known, fully loved babies dancing around the screen. I was euphoric.

At the end of the scan, I texted Zach, "All done. Two perfect babies!" because I didn't know that "I'm going to show these to the doctor and see if she has anything to say" meant "Something is terribly, tragically wrong."

The tech poked her head in a few minutes later and told me I should get my husband on the phone. Instantly, all the joy and peace I'd felt over the past couple of hours were sucked out of my body. I was hollow. I was empty. I was going to throw up.

My hands shook as I FaceTimed Zach. He was moving the trailer to a different site that day, and all the kids were with him in the truck. He tried to quiet them so he could hear what was going on—not an easy feat, between his terrible cell service and the hospital's unreliable Wi-Fi.

I sat on the crispy paper covering the bed, clenching the stack of ultrasound pictures. "Something's wrong," I told him anxiously. "I don't know what. I saw their hearts beating. I don't think the scan would have lasted two hours if they were dead. I don't know. I don't know."

Zach's eyebrows furrowed. He handed the kids their iPads and stepped out of the truck. His voice was breaking in and out, and I was close to breaking down. The room felt so cold. The paper was so dry. The lights were so bright. The mask across my mouth was suffocating me. I wanted to vomit. I wanted to run. I wanted to die. Something was really, really wrong.

Later that day, back in my in-laws' house, I tried to make sense of the news we'd received. *Two babies, but only one could survive and I had to choose which one.*

I lay on the futon in a fetal position, my arms wrapped tightly around my belly, and tried to process the impossible. How had things changed so much—and so quickly? How do we go from budgeting for diapers to not knowing if we're even going to need them?

A futon in my in-laws' basement in snowy Massachusetts was a far cry from the life of adventure and sun we'd been living for the past year. I felt every bit of the weight of what was happening. I was raw from crying. I'd shed more tears in the last six hours than I had in years. I was crippled by fear.

When I couldn't form another thought in my mind and was left with only raw emotion, I looked up to the ceiling and whispered, "I'm so tired of being a test subject for your faithfulness."

I'd been through so much already. I'd already experienced so much pain and loss and heartbreak. And now here we were: after years of trying to have a baby, we were thrown into the shadow of death once again.

I was tired. This felt like an unnecessary plot twist. I had nothing to prove to God, and he had nothing to prove to me. I no longer believed that suffering was punishment or proof that I was in the will of God or something given simply to teach us something. I believed that suffering was an inevitable part of being a human, and I believed that God was with us, fully present in our suffering, offering comfort throughout it.

In that moment when our pregnancy turned high risk, my theology was jolted from the theoretical to the practical. Would I choose to trust that God was who I believed him to be? When the doctors told us that the only option to save one of our babies was to end the life of the other one, we had to quickly determine how strongly we believed in God's goodness and sovereignty. If we really believed that only God is the author and finisher of life, we would have to place both our daughters' lives in his hands, trusting that he is good, no matter the outcome. Did we believe this enough to risk both of their lives? Did I believe it enough to bear my convictions with my actual body?

THE DISTORTION:
Questioning what I believe about God
will cause my faith to become fragile.

❁

THE SHIFT:
When crisis reveals my incomplete theology,
my questions are an invitation to know God better.

3

When There's
No Good Choice

He who learns must suffer. And even in our sleep pain that cannot
forget falls drop by drop upon the heart, and in our own despair,
against our will, comes wisdom to us by the awful grace of God.

AESCHYLUS

IN EVERY COLLEGE ETHICS CLASS, some version of this scenario is
given: two children are stuck on the train tracks. Their mother is
close by and has only enough time to save one. Which child should
she choose?

Sometimes more information is given: one child is sick and has
a fatal diagnosis. One child is rebellious and makes the mother's
life miserable. One child is not her biological child at all. All these
details are supposed to make the choice more complicated, or perhaps easier. Everyone rationalizes a different decision based on
what the mother would value most. It's a scenario that isn't likely
to happen to anyone in the room and doesn't serve a purpose other
than intellectual stimulation and a hypothetical ethics debate.

But I actually lived it.

The problem was Baby B's cord. She was experiencing something called absent cord flow. This happens when the blood going from the placenta to the umbilical cord and into the baby's body doesn't flow as consistently as it should. Instead of providing a steady stream of blood, Baby B's cord flowed and stopped and then flowed again. When the steady flow began again after stopping, it caused blood to surge into her body.

While typical umbilical-cord blood flow is like a river, hers was more like waves in an ocean. The major risk was that the absent flow would become reverse flow, where the blood flows from the placenta, stops, and then goes back to the placenta. Baby B's blood flow was never consistent—sometimes it was intermittently absent; other times it was persistently absent, but never what was considered normal.

If Baby B's blood flow became reverse, it could stop her heart. This would send a surge of blood through the shared placenta into Baby A's heart.

Our options were limited. The doctors laid out a few possible diagnoses, but there weren't enough compounding issues to make an official conclusion. One week we were given a diagnosis of selective intrauterine growth restriction (sIUGR). The next week it was borderline twin to twin transfusion (TTTS). Other times it was simply the absent blood flow.

Zach and I were presented with three options. We could do nothing, hoping the babies would survive but putting them both at risk of dying. Or I could have a surgery that would separate the babies' placenta into two, giving each of them half a placenta to live on. This would protect Baby A from the effects of Baby B's potential death but would limit the nutrients both babies would receive from the placenta, putting them at risk for brain injury, other developmental complications, and death. Or we could terminate Baby B, eliminating all the risks for Baby A and have a healthy pregnancy and full-term birth with Baby A.

The final risk analysis related to my own life. Carrying twins, no matter what type, can be brutal on a woman's body, but carrying twins who share a placenta increases the risk of preeclampsia, a blood pressure condition that's potentially fatal for the mother. Deciding to carry both babies as long as possible was a risk not only to their lives but to my own.

At our first scan, when the doctor left the room after giving me the fatal diagnosis, I turned my phone to face me. Zach and I just stared at each other in shock. Neither of us knew what to say.

With tears streaming down my face, I finally said, "There's no decision. We can't abort Baby B. We can't do that."

He just nodded his head. "Okay."

I wish I could say, "And that was that!" And I guess in some ways it was. We never changed our minds. But every week after that, from nineteen to twenty-six weeks pregnant, I was presented with the option of terminating Baby B to save Baby A. At each appointment, the doctors explained the scenario with different reasoning. First they recommended terminating Baby B to save Baby A's life. Then they advised us to terminate Baby B to save Baby A's quality of life.

My doctor explained that if Baby A survived Baby B's death, the blood surge to her heart could cause her to have a stroke, resulting in brain injury. It could also lead to an emergency C-section and hyper-prematurity, which could result in developmental delays, blindness, deafness, or paralysis. There was no shortage of risks. "If you really care about the quality of Baby A's life," the doctor said, "you'll need to terminate B."

I hated having to repeat our choice over and over again. At one point, I was having three scans a week. I had to choose every time, three times a week, to not abort one of our babies to save the other. It was emotional agony to have to choose over and over again which child should live. The choice was mine—but was it really? What kind of choice is that?

I wonder if it would have been easier if we'd only had to make the decision once. But one of the more complicated pieces of our story is the reality that by deciding not to abort one baby, we knowingly put the other at risk.

Baby B's life was a direct threat to Baby A's. We knew that. And yet we decided to risk it. We were sure about our choice, but it didn't come easily. And it was a choice we had to keep making until the day termination was no longer an option in our state. Every week—multiple times a week—I had to choose to risk Baby A's life for the chance of holding them both.

But it wasn't much of a choice at all. One of my friends would later describe it as "making a forward motion under duress." We were just taking one step forward. And then another. And another. How does a mother choose which child to save? It's every parent's worst nightmare, and it was my waking one.

❋

In 1 Kings, there's a story about a baby and two women who claimed to be his mother. The baby was brought to King Solomon, and in an epic custody battle, King Solomon offered to solve the problem by cutting the baby in half and giving each mother one half.

One of the women said, "Yeah, okay, fine."

But the other said, "No! Just let her have him—don't kill him."

And that's how King Solomon decided who the real mother was.

I've always thought that was such a strange story. Surely there had to be another way to determine who the real mother was, right? Why was Solomon's immediate thought, *Let me offer to cut the baby in half. That'll shake out the real mother.*

What?

I always side-eyed that story, taking it at face value and never thinking too much about it. But when I reread the story while everything was happening with our girls, I saw myself in it for the first time.

In those hospital rooms, when I was faced with the most impossible choice, I was both the mother and the king. I was the king holding the sword, the fate of the child in my hands. And I was the mother, with no control.

If I decided anything, it was simply to not wield the sword. But in making that choice, I was deciding to put our healthy baby's life at risk, out of the slim hope that I would get to keep them both. Their futures were in our hands, and we had to decide whose life had more value and what *kind* of life had more value.

We hoped and we prayed and we believed that it would be okay. We were confident that the only choice we could make was to trust their lives to the hands of God. But we didn't feel good about it. There was zero joy in that choice. In that moment, there was no decision we could have made that would have felt good.

But we chose. Even in chaos, wisdom was available to us. Our certainty in the decision came from our deeply rooted beliefs about who God is, what his Word says, and what we believed about life, creation, and God's sovereignty. To take either one of our babies' lives in our hands and make a decision about who goes and who stays would have been a violation of what we believed.

> Even in chaos, wisdom was available to us.

When we shared parts of our story, some people tried to co-opt our experience for their particular ideology. But pigeonholing our situation into a talking point only diminished how sacred a choice this was for us. We didn't choose not to terminate because of our ideology. We weren't rallying on any political hills.

When pro-choicers said to me, "Well, aren't you glad you had the *choice?*" I responded with: "I should have only had to choose once, but that wasn't enough. I had to repeat my choice over and over and over again." I do understand that this is what had to be done—the doctors had no choice but to present the options to me at every appointment. My frustration with these comments was more about the disregard for the emotional toll it took on me to continually make this decision.

When pro-lifers elevated me as a model of bravery, I asked, "What's the most pro-life thing I can do? Terminating one baby would save both my life and the other baby's life. By not terminating, I'm actually putting us all at more risk. I'm gambling with their lives. That isn't very pro-life of me."

Decisions can't be made on ideological hills, and ideologies alone don't hold up in a doctor's office or when tragedy is staring you down. When you're facing an impossible choice, it's not enough to ask yourself if your decision matches up with your worldview. It's much more personal and immediate than that. You have to ask yourself, *What decision honors what I believe to be true about my Creator?*

If I believed that God was the author and creator of life, then how would I honor him in this fragile situation? If I believed that he was in control, that he was sovereign, and that he was trustworthy, was my trust in him enough to let me walk away from the guarantee of one child and risk losing both my daughters?

The most important decisions of our lives aren't based only on what we believe but on how much we actually believe it. When I was given a sword and told to choose a baby, my beliefs about God's design and his sovereignty over life and death had already formed deeply in my heart. I pointed the sword away from my babies and toward myself, willing to bear the physical and emotional scars, because I believe that God is the author of all life. If I had been standing only on an ideological hill, I might have chosen differently. When our hearts are deeply formed by our connection to the Father, our choices reflect that.

It's hard to make decisions when your ears are ringing. Crisis is like a cast-iron pan to your head. It makes your brain spiral into chaos and confusion. How can a person be expected to make good decisions when all the circuits of their brain have short-circuited and been rewired?

But even in the chaos, wisdom is accessible to us. Even when we feel helpless, there are decisions that are ours to make. Even when things are happening outside our control, we can be intentional about exerting the will God has given us.

We all have a framework for the way we make decisions, even if it isn't something we've consciously thought through. Maybe you make a list, or maybe there are specific people you talk to. Maybe you have a system for praying, fasting, and listening to Jesus. Or maybe you're impulsive and you've never thought through a thing a day in your life, and it's worked out for you so far. That makes me a little sweaty to think about, but hey, that's great for you! Whatever your processes, we all have them. Thankfully, our decisions aren't usually emergencies. Most days, we don't wake up in a life-or-death situation that requires us to make a judgment call in a hurry. We can take our time, weigh our options, and make a well-researched, thought-through, prayed-over choice.

Life can be sort of random, and sometimes we find ourselves in the middle of chaos, trying to make decisions that will change the entire trajectory of our lives. Some of us get a little too confident in our decision-making frameworks, because they've never steered us wrong—ever!

But sometimes a storm throws our ship onto the waves while simultaneously smashing our compass. Things settle down, as things tend to do, and we're left without a guide to point us in the right direction. How will we decide which direction to swim when we don't know where the shore is anymore?

※

The year after we left full-time pastoral ministry, on the heels of a painful split with the leadership at our church, Zach and I decided to move to a dangerous neighborhood in our city. Looking back, I think part of the reason was that we were trying to make sense of why we felt so strongly that God had called us to this city only to be cast out of the community and job that had brought us there.

We didn't feel like God had released us from the city. We still believed this was where we were supposed to live. But we also knew we weren't supposed to be in full-time career ministry anymore. So where did that leave us? We thought, *Well, maybe God is calling us to actually be in the city. The scary parts. The parts people like us usually avoided.*

Leaving our church had turned our framework for ministry inside out, and we were still trying to figure out what it meant to be called by God if we weren't employed in that calling. It was messy, and we were figuring it out as we went.

We didn't think it made sense to minister in the inner city if we weren't willing to live there, so we moved into a neighborhood knowing it wasn't safe. We just didn't know *how* unsafe it was. We didn't know there was a gang named after the street we lived on. We didn't know we were living above and next door to notorious gang members. They were just our neighbors, and we liked them. We were naive and idealistic. But we did the best with the information we had, and we moved in with our hopes high. We didn't have a ministry plan or a list of directives. We just wanted to be good neighbors and wait for the Holy Spirit to direct our steps.

We got used to hearing gunshots in the area, and we knew not to stay near the windows or linger at our car. But other than taking precautions just in case something were to happen nearby, we didn't have much reason to think we weren't safe.

But one day we were in the car turning down our street, and I heard the Lord speak in an undeniable way: *Don't go home.*

The words felt heavy and convincing, like someone had jumped in front of my face and screamed them at me. I placed one hand on the middle console next to me and the other hand on the passenger door, as if bracing myself. It felt like something was about to happen.

I stared straight ahead, and just as we were about to turn into the driveway, I said, "Don't go home."

Zach turned to me. "Huh?"

I started to panic. "Don't go home, don't go home, don't go home." I couldn't explain it, but I just knew we had to get out of danger.

After we drove away, I felt a little silly. Of course, we needed to go home. It was our home. But we couldn't. I didn't know why— I just knew we couldn't.

We stayed away until I felt the pressure on my chest ease up. I told Zach that I thought it would be safe now, and we drove home.

As we pulled into our driveway, a young guy was walking down the driveway of our home and then turned onto the sidewalk out front.

I made eye contact with him and then looked at his hands. He had brass knuckles across each of his fingers and the unmistakable outline of a gun in his pants. I don't know what God protected us from that day, but seeing that boy walk down our street equipped for violence told me everything I needed to know. We weren't safe. I knew that now.

That night, Zach and I talked about our priorities and what we were willing to risk to do this "life as ministry" thing we had idealized. Were we so sure that this was what God was calling us to do that we were willing to sacrifice the safety of our family to do it?

We considered that it might be time to think about moving but shelved the conversation for another day. Our usual process was to pray, listen to Jesus, seek wise counsel, and then come together again and make a decision. We didn't want to procrastinate and risk something happening, but we weren't necessarily in a rush. We thought we had some time to make sure we were making a wise choice.

A few days later, we ran out of time.

It was one of the first warm spring days in Massachusetts, and I was setting up my office on the second floor of our apartment while Zach and the kids, ages seven, five, and four, played in the backyard.

We never let the kids wander anywhere but the backyard, because our friend, a detective in the city, had recently warned us to not let them run around in the front.

"Because people speed down the street?" I'd asked.

"Because of stray bullets."

We took him seriously and played only in the back.

Zach was leaving for work, so he brought the kids in and kissed us goodbye. Then I set the kids up with some cardboard boxes to play with while I organized my office.

They were in the room next to me, making castles and forts for less than ten minutes, when I heard gunshots. They sounded closer than ever before.

When I looked out my window, I froze. As soon as I registered what was happening, I ran into the next room and grabbed all three kids. I pulled them onto the ground next to me and held them as far away from the windows as we could get. Their eyes were locked on mine, looking to me to tell them how to feel.

We stared at each other breathlessly for what felt like ages but was probably just a minute. I held them close to me, and they craned their necks to watch my face.

The chaos was unfolding immediately outside our window, so we heard every crack of the gun, every footstep on concrete, every scream, every squeal of tires.

Seconds after the gunshots stopped, the screaming started. "Who was that?" I heard my neighbor scream. "Who was that!" "Call 911!" someone else shouted.

I ran to the window and saw the lifeless form of my neighbor's friend, his bloody body face down, just a few feet from where my kids had been playing minutes earlier.

The backyard hadn't been safe either. We'd escaped the path of death by just a few minutes.

I panicked. "That could have been them," I said out loud. "That could have been my kids."

I called Zach. No answer. *What do I do. What do I do.*

More screaming. More yelling. It sounded like a crowd was gathering outside. *Are we safe?*

I pictured my unlocked back door, the stairs leading directly to the room we were in. *What if the shooter tries to hide? What if he comes inside? We're stuck. We're stuck here.*

I called Zach's brother, who lived a few streets away, and he came to pick us up. I ran from my house with my kids, all of us barefoot and terrified. As we rushed to his car, I glanced back and saw that our house and our neighbor's house were being taped off with crime-scene tape.

Word traveled quickly to our family and friends. "Kristen just saw someone get killed."

The shock rippled through our community, and the panicked calls started coming in. Out of love for us and fear for our family, they were compelled to share their opinions and advice about what we should do next.

My phone buzzed with text messages and calls, one after the other, without breaks, for hours. Everyone wanted to know if we were okay. They wanted to know what we were going to do.

I couldn't get the images and sounds of what I'd just experienced out of my head, much less process whether we should move or stay.

Someone would say, "You have to leave. You can't go back."

And I'd hear the echoes of gunshots: *BANG, BANG, BANG, BANG.*

"You guys can't just move! It's your home!"

Who was that? WHO WAS THAT!

"You shouldn't even go back to pack your things."

Someone call 911!

"Neighborhoods like that need people like you. Don't let the gangs win!"

BANG, BANG, BANG, BANG.

I couldn't hear what anyone was saying. I couldn't make sense of what I'd just seen and heard and felt. How were we supposed to go home when our home was a crime scene? How were we supposed to make a decision when our bodies were in flight?

We decided our focus had to be on our small children and making sure they felt safe and protected. We needed to tend to our family before we rushed to a decision. Everything else and everyone else could wait.

My sons, ages seven and five, attached themselves to my side. They repeated things like "I'll keep you safe, Mom. I'll protect you."

Friends surrounded us with love and support. They offered meals and warm beds, and they watched our kids so Zach and I could talk without having them in earshot. We tried to censor our words around them so they wouldn't know what I'd seen outside our window. I don't think they knew someone was murdered, but they knew I was scared. They knew something bad had happened.

I stopped answering calls and responding to texts. I shut off my phone completely. I couldn't hear one more word of advice, no matter how well-meaning it was. All I knew was that I could no longer hear my own thoughts.

You'd think this decision would be a no-brainer, right? Someone was murdered next to our house, and we were thinking about going back? But our framework for decision-making wasn't just about evaluating circumstances. The question we were asking wasn't just *Are we safe?* but *What does God have for us?* We had to drown out the other voices so we could hear him above the chaos. We wanted our decision to be intentional, not reactionary.

The best advice came from my older brother, who said, "Don't leave because you're scared. Don't stay because you feel guilty."

A few days after the shooting, my friend—the wife of the detective who had warned us about stray bullets—called me. "I have some really bad news. I'm so sorry, Kristen. But you can't go home. It isn't safe."

She was right. Two weeks later, on the same day we moved our final things out of the house, our downstairs neighbor was wounded in a shooting on our front steps. Our neighbor from across the street texted us photos of the ambulance in our driveway and the cops lined up on our street. Our former home was taped off in crime-scene tape. Again.

Making decisions in the middle of a traumatic event is a practice in "doing the next thing," as the old poem says.* There are times when something happens and you don't have the luxury of

---

* *Popularized by Elisabeth Elliot, the anonymous poem reads, in part, "In His dear presence, the rest of His calm/The light of His countenance be thy psalm/Strong in His faithfulness, praise and sing/Then, as He beckons thee, do the next thing."*

making a pro/con list. You don't have time to pray, fast, or seek wise counsel from trusted mentors. You just have to rely on the information you have and trust that the Holy Spirit will give you enough guidance to go on.

When you're in trauma, you can barely do more than replay the events over and over as you process and try to make sense of what happened. Advice, however well intended, is not likely to be absorbed in the first moments, first days, or first weeks after a traumatic event.

Our brains literally can't reason following trauma; they're just surviving. This is true in obvious crises like witnessing a murder, being physically abused or sexually assaulted, getting in a serious car accident, or losing a loved one. But it also happens in the more misunderstood traumas like being hurt by a spiritual community, experiencing emotional or spiritual abuse, or being in proximity to someone who has experienced trauma. Everyone responds differently to crisis, but trauma of any kind makes it difficult to function at even a basic level.

When you're a believer and trauma enters your life, it doesn't just shake your faith, which would result in enough chaos in itself. It also dismantles your entire framework for living.

Having a decision-making framework is helpful, because it guides you as you're making choices when you can barely string two thoughts together. But it's hard to make decisions when your framework revolves around your faith and you're not sure what you believe or who you can trust anymore. When the framework is broken, so is your process for making decisions. When this happens, not only are you replaying the traumatic event and trying to make sense of it, but you're also trying to make crucial, life-altering decisions for yourself and your family.

When we split from our church community, the decision-making framework we'd relied on became completely irrelevant.

We didn't know who we could trust. We didn't trust ourselves, and we were holding on to our trust in God by a thin thread. In an instant, we had to find new jobs and a new place to live, and we had to make a complete lifestyle change. We were in so much pain, and yet we had to think practically and logistically about finding a home and a way to provide for our three small children.

When our pregnancy turned crisis, we weren't able to make the kind of educated decision we normally would. There just wasn't time. Whenever we were faced with a choice, we had to decide quickly and confidently. Without a framework, we were just making our best guesses and hoping it would be all right.

How do you weigh spiritual factors in your choices when you no longer have mentors you can trust for guidance? How do you think practically when your emotions are prone to spiral at any given moment—for any reason, or for no reason at all? How do you find your way when you don't know where you are in a world that is completely unrecognizable? How do you listen for how God is leading you when you don't trust him anymore?

Most of the time, making decisions while in crisis is like waking up in a room you've never been in before, with all the lights off. You're trying to find your way out without so much as the flashlight on your phone.

You lose all sense of direction. You don't know who to ask for help. Even if you find someone, you don't know what to ask for. Sometimes you don't even know that you can ask at all. You're lost, spiraling, desperate for a hand to hold but not sure who you can trust.

Crisis removes both foresight and hindsight, so all we have to go on is what's right in front of us, moment to moment. It's absolutely terrifying to need to make a decision and not know how to do it, much less what to decide. But it isn't hopeless. We aren't doomed to navigate traumatic events without a compass.

When our lives are thrown into chaos, sometimes, the only guidance we have is the Spirit and the anchors that hold our faith. Without those deeply planted anchors, we'll find ourselves flailing, trying to hold on to anything we can wrap our hands around. We'll struggle to make decisions that are right and wise for ourselves and our families.

Suffering of any kind can cause both a practical crisis and a spiritual crisis. In the practical, you have to decide how you're going to respond to your situation and how it affects your day-to-day life. What will you do about your living situation, your relationships, your ability to bring an income to your family? There are a million details that come front and center when your world is turned upside down, and you have to try to navigate these complexities with a sound mind, even when your world is spinning off its axis.

In the spiritual, you have to decide how you're going to respond to your suffering and how it will inform your faith and your worldview. In the midst of crisis, you're confronted with your view of God, suffering, the church, and your very salvation. Pain has a way of confronting your theology. Even when you aren't consciously thinking about it, your mind and your spirit are responding to the questions and doubts unearthed by your pain.

The book of Proverbs is full of verses that call for us to seek wisdom and hold on to it. Wisdom is often personified as a woman (a point that I lovingly make to my husband, lest he question my decision-making abilities), and we are invited to pursue wisdom, hold on to her, not abandon her, and trust that she will guide us well. Proverbs 4:6 says that if you love wisdom, "she will guard you."* Proverbs 8:12 says that wisdom shares a home with shrewdness and has knowledge and discretion.

---

* CSB

Throughout Scripture, we see that wisdom is readily available and accessible to us, if only we ask. Sometimes wisdom is gained through the very experiences we need wisdom to navigate. The Lord's wisdom will guide us, even when we're without our normal navigation systems.

Theology is studied in textbooks, but it's formed in deep valleys of pain and suffering. We can quote doctrines and creeds, but it's in the moments when that theology has a heartbeat and a name that you're shown what you truly believe.

In a hospital room, facing the impossible situation of choosing one child over the other, my theology had beating hearts.

> Theology is studied in textbooks, but it's formed in deep valleys of pain and suffering.

But my choice was so much more than choosing who would live or die. I also had to decide if I believed my convictions enough to risk their lives. I laid my sword on the altar of my theology and trusted that God would provide a ram.

In our suffering, we are given the gift of twofold wisdom: first, the wisdom to navigate what we're walking through in the moment, and second, the wisdom we gain from walking through it. The wisdom we gain allows us to drop anchors, reminding us of where we've been and how the Lord has steadied us in previous storms.

The anchors of our faith give us both clarity and hope when our hearts are so heavy that every beat is a shock. We can't imagine that our heart will keep beating, yet every moment, it dares to keep us alive. When we're too weak to do more than put one foot in front of the other, the anchors we hold on to will keep us steady. We might not know what will happen next, but we know what—and in whom—we believe.

All of us have been, or will be, violently tossed by the waves of heartache. We get caught in the storm and don't know what to do next because we don't know how to choose or who to trust. We don't know where we are in a world that's suddenly become unrecognizable. But it's in the sinking of our ship that we find the anchors and the compass we need to hold steady and navigate our lives.

The next time a storm comes, it won't knock us out of the boat. We'll know what our anchors are so we can hold on for dear life when that's all we can do.

THE DISTORTION:
I'm not capable of making good
decisions when I'm suffering.

THE SHIFT:
Wisdom is available to me,
no matter what's happening around me.

4

The Darkness of the Valley

I used to think that grief was about looking backward, old men saddled
with regrets or young ones pondering should-haves. I see now that it
is about eyes squinting through tears into an unbearable future.

KATE BOWLER

THE NIGHT OF OUR DAUGHTERS' DIAGNOSIS, I barely slept. I
groaned and tossed and turned and woke up every hour, hoping it
wasn't real, and then groaned again until I fell back asleep. It was
the most primal prayer a mother can pray. It filled every bone,
every muscle, every artery, every ventricle. The very marrow of my
body was filled with the prayer of a mother staring down the barrel
of a gun pointed at her children.

Mine were prayers that contained no words and yet contained
all words. I was experiencing what Paul wrote about: "In the same
way the Spirit also helps us in our weakness, because we do not
know what to pray for as we should, but the Spirit himself inter-
cedes for us with inexpressible groanings."*

Romans 8:26, CSB

The morning after the diagnosis, the reality of our situation started to sink in. It was real now. Maybe that sounds a little silly—of course it was real. But everything was moving so fast and it felt so chaotic that I seemed to be floating somewhere above it all. All this had been happening to me and around me, but it wasn't happening *in* me yet. I was standing still on a moving floor.

After a night of my spirit battling while my body tried to sleep, the morning felt offensive. As the sun crept up, letting cracks of light into the bedroom, it illuminated a reality I would have rather forgotten. There was comfort in the darkness. In the light, I had to face what was happening.

I was hopeful but heavy. Every moment had weight to it, and I was painfully aware of how fragile our situation was. I was moving cautiously, convinced that any misstep would fracture this balance between life and death.

I don't really know how to describe what it feels like to walk through the valley of the shadow of death. Words inevitably fail, because there are no metaphors or analogies or poetic phrasings that accurately describe it—and I'm not sure I'd even want to if I could.

All I can say is that it's a place of fear: thick, tangible, mocking fear. Even though I felt hopeful that my babies would be okay, their deaths seemed a breath away. There were days when I felt death sitting on my shoulder, smirking at my optimism and reminding me how little control I had.

I knew my daughters could die. I hoped they wouldn't, but I knew they could. Not just that they *could*, but that they likely *would*. I'd done enough research on mono-dichorionic twin pregnancies to know that the chances of this ending the way we wanted it to were slim. The reality was that we were likely to lose both our babies.

It's dark there in the valley.

Throughout that first day, the messages, texts, and emails came flooding in from all over the world. Our story was going viral on Instagram, and thousands of people were praying for a miracle. The overall theme of the prayers was that God would spare our daughters' lives so the world would see a real miracle. People said things like "God, use these girls to show your glory!" And "Give this family victory so the world can see how good you are!"

I understood what they meant. I've done my fair share of bargaining with God, reminding him who he is and what a victory would mean for the church and the world. Those prayers are a desperate begging under the delusion that God needs to do something for me to get something for himself.

Sometimes we fancy ourselves as God's publicity agents, leveraging suffering for a divine marketing moment. "Look at what this good thing will mean for your image, God! Look how many people will believe in you if you do this!"

When we encounter suffering in the life of someone who loves Jesus, we assume God can only be glorified if the outcome lands in our favor. The only kind of marketing we'll accept is a victory that can be seen and felt.

Within the church, we don't see much value in miracles that aren't loud. What good is a victory if it isn't packaged, marketed, and sold to the highest bidder for the Kingdom of God?

But a victory can still be good even if it's quiet, even if the only people who ever know about it are the ones who experienced it. It's small of us to believe that all the good things God has done have to be put on display for the world to consume. It's even smaller of us to believe that the only good things worthy of being displayed are the victories we've prayed for.

I know that the prayers and messages sent for us were genuine, and I believe that the Lord heard them and received them. But that day, as I heard prayer after prayer demanding a victory so God could be glorified, I thought, *No, no, no. God doesn't owe me this.*

I saw the reality of our circumstances and thought about this practically. I thought about what it would mean if all these people begged God for a miracle and I publicly aligned with the "Do this, so that . . ." model of prayer, and then one (or both) of my babies died. Would thousands of people lose their faith because we collectively prayed for a good thing to happen and it didn't? Would bringing so many people into my story be the catalyst for a crisis in someone else's life?

I couldn't live with that. I wanted everyone to know that I didn't feel like God owed me a victory. I asked myself, *Will God still be glorified in this if things don't go our way? What if . . . he doesn't?*

Because sometimes he doesn't.

I know that life has not given me all the grief I'll ever experience. I'm still young, and it would be naive of me to believe that the saddest parts of my life are behind me. One day I may look back on my reflections on this experience and think, *Oh, honey, what do you know about this?* But the worst thing you've ever been through is still the worst thing you've ever been through. And while time will likely present more and different griefs than I've experienced up to now, I strongly believe that we should honor the grief we know and not dismiss its impact on us.

Sometimes we experience pain that is so acute, its sting stays with us, no matter how much time passes. My miscarriage has been like that for me. It's a grief that had no victory, and it holds a sacred place in my heart.

A year and a half before we found out we were pregnant with the girls, we found out we were pregnant with our fourth baby.

We hadn't been trying for very long and I hadn't been pregnant for very long, but we were so excited.

The miscarriage itself took days. At first, we were sure we were losing the baby, and then we weren't so sure. We thought maybe it was a false alarm and it would be okay, but it wasn't. My pregnancy ended with me in a fetal position, bleeding and moaning on the bathroom floor. A few hours later, I began to hemorrhage and had to have an emergency D&C to remove the remaining tissue in my uterus.

Our children grieved as children do—by drawing pictures and processing their emotions out loud—without the softening of words we learn as adults. They named the baby Max, and we began the slow process of moving forward together.

For the next week or so, I couldn't move more than a few steps at a time. Grief and anemia do not make good companions.

My sister and I had been pregnant together, due within days of each other. We're eight years apart, and neither of us thought we'd be pregnant at the same time. But we were . . . and then we weren't.

She was sensitive to my loss and careful in the way she shared her pregnancy with me. I held my joy for her and my grief for myself in separate hands. The reality is, we both lost something when my baby died.

A few weeks before she was due, my sister and her husband moved in with us temporarily. She delivered her beautiful baby girl in the same hospital where my pregnancy had ended. I held one of her knees during labor. It was beautiful and it was brutal.

We didn't get to hold our baby, but I was happy she was able to hold hers.

Having a newborn in our home the same week we would have had our own newborn was a kind of good that's hard to explain. It wasn't healing in the sense that it filled the void the loss of our baby left, but it was healing in the way all good things are. Like the way a sunny day feels after weeks of clouds and rain.

There's nothing that comforts my grief over the loss of our baby, even now, years later. One of my friends who has gone through a miscarriage said that having another baby didn't fix the grief, but it did dull it. It hasn't been like that for me. There was enough time between when our baby would have been due and when I got pregnant with the girls that I was never able to comfort myself by saying, "If we'd had that baby, we wouldn't have the girls!" We had room for them all.

I will always yearn to have all my kids with me on this side of heaven, and I will never have that.

I've heard older moms say that the way to know if you're done having children is to picture your dinner table twenty years from now. "Are the kids you have right now the only kids at the table? If you're picturing more children in twenty years, you're not done yet!"

My table will never be full. There will always be an empty chair. No number of children I can birth will change that. Max will always be gone. My table will never be full.

I don't find comfort in knowing Max is waiting for us in heaven—it just isn't tangible for me. I loved him on earth, and I want him on earth. Heaven is too abstract when it comes to addressing gaping wounds in the soul.

And *how* is he waiting for us in heaven? Did he skip past the seven more months of gestation needed to become a fully formed newborn, just waiting for me in the afterlife? How does that work? How can I imagine a face I never saw? This doesn't comfort me; it makes me ache even more.

Even if he doesn't. And he didn't.

It has felt cruel and unfair and unkind. What good can be drawn from losing a baby? Trying to pull good from such a loss is insulting. How can someone look at my devastation and say it was good? For whom? Because for me, it's been persistent heartache.

I don't want to be relieved of my pain—it's all I have of him. It's all that connects me to the baby I never got to hold. All I have is the grief that tethers me to a child who was made from love and who was instantly loved and who was never held by that love on this side of heaven. Where is the comfort for hearts like mine that ache for something we never really knew but lost just the same?

The comfort of "even if he doesn't" isn't just that one day he will, which I fully believe. It's that he's good anyway. He's faithful anyway. He's just anyway. He's loving anyway. Even when he doesn't.

The pain we experience might cause us to see God in a different way. And it makes sense, because we can't look at our pain objectively, as if it weren't happening to us. When we experience loss and grief, we aren't able to think rationally; we're just trying to survive. So of course we look toward heaven and cry, "How could you?" There isn't anything wrong with that.

When you find yourself in a grief so deep that it turns your heart toward accusations and anger at God, remember that you're in good company. David, Job, Jonah, and Jesus (to name a few)* all turned their faces to their Father and said the same thing: "How could you?" But his character doesn't alter just because our perception of him does.

We praise the faith of those who believe in the goodness of God even when things don't go their way. When you can stand on the battleground of your life, surrounded by death and destruction, and say, "I still believe he's good, even though he didn't," the crowd will be in awe of your strength and fortitude. The church will be

---

* Each prayer is different, but prayers of lament are common throughout Scripture, including one from Jesus, who cried out the Psalm 22 lament "My God, my God, why have you forsaken me?" See also Psalm 10:1; 13:1; Job 7:20; Habakkuk 1:2; and Matthew 27:46.

inspired and challenged, and they'll wonder if their faith is made of whatever yours is made of.

They see your faith as loud and brave and bold, but they don't see your shaky legs. They don't know that when you said, "Even though he didn't," it was barely a whisper. That's enough, though. If a whisper of faith is all you've got, a whisper of faith is all you need.

Sometimes he doesn't. But sometimes he does.

And when he does, the joy is in the answered prayer—but it's also in knowing that even though he didn't have to, he did. What a joy it is to be the recipient of a miracle when you know the pain of a tragedy. What a grace it is to believe that he's good even if he doesn't, but he still does. He doesn't have anything to prove to you, but he does it anyway.

❋

The day after our world imploded at our twenty-week ultrasound, I borrowed my mother-in-law's car and drove two hours to my brother's house in New Hampshire. I pressed play on a playlist I'd made called "Hope" and turned the volume high enough to drown out the sound of my crying and screaming.

I could feel both of my babies turning and kicking in my stomach, and I hoped that my moans and my cries would be enough for God to turn his ear toward me. The words *What if he doesn't?* were bouncing around the walls of my head, and my ears were ringing. I needed to speak.

I pulled over at a rest area in Vermont, set my phone on my steering wheel, and spoke to my Instagram following for the first time since the doctor's appointment.

It felt sacred, in a way, to be able to communicate what was in my heart and head in the middle of so much uncertainty. I talked about times when God hadn't done what I'd prayed he would do and how he was good anyway. He was faithful anyway. He was glorified anyway. None of my bargaining chips had worked, but he was still good, even in my pain.

I took a deep breath and said, "Even if he doesn't make things go our way, I'll still believe that he's good and kind and faithful. Even if he doesn't."

Later, while reflecting on that moment with my mom, she said, "When you took that breath, it was like I was watching your faith rise from your belly and out of your mouth." That's what it felt like for me too. Not that my faith was built in that moment, but that it was exposed in it. It came from the faith that God would be good, regardless, and the peace that even if he didn't save our daughters' lives, I would be okay. Heartbroken, of course, but okay.

I think it's a theological red flag when we are consistently surprised by the kindness of God. We are so ready to accept his judgment and punishment that we're caught off guard by his grace. We often miss it because we tend to associate heavenly good with earthly good. Sometimes the two are aligned and what we want is what God gives us, but other times the goodness in our lives can't be measured by the stick we hold up to it.

There's no formula to calculate God's goodness in our lives. It's nice to think that if we do this and that, God will protect us, bless us, and make things go our way. But why do we think we can put God on our leash? Who are we to think we have God figured out? Why do we try to make him small enough to fit a formula that makes sense to *us*?

We're called to seek Christ for who he is, not for what we can get from him. We aren't entitled to have every prayer answered, and we aren't promised a life of ease. But God is also really kind and merciful and gracious, and I don't think it's absurd to want him to be all of those things to you.

If a child were telling you about his dad and said, "Yeah, he doesn't really talk to me, and sometimes he's kind of mean, but that's okay. He doesn't need to show me that he loves me. I just know that he does." You would (hopefully) respond with anger and grief over the lack of love and attachment in this child's life. Children deserve to be loved and cared for and to be shown that love and care. We aren't born instinctively knowing that we're loved. That love needs to be expressed to us—by our earthly parents and our heavenly Father.

The prosperity gospel would have us believe we can manipulate the hand of God to bring material, tangible blessings. But the reality is that God can't be manipulated, so that's a fail from the start. We don't have to manipulate God to give us good things—he already wants to give them to us. When we approach the throne, we can do so with boldness, humility, and awe. His character doesn't change, and neither does his love for you.

Sometimes God shows his love in ways that we ask for, and other times his love feels like he's taking a wrecking ball to our lives. When I look back at some of the things that have made me angry and bitter toward God, it's only with time and perspective that I can say, "Oh, he was actually rescuing me, but I couldn't see it then. I thought I was in a hot tub, but I was the frog in the pot, not realizing I was slowly boiling to death. God scooped me out just in time." Now, instead of feeling anger, I can look back with gratitude that he saw what I couldn't see and allowed me to hurt for a while, but he didn't let me die. God didn't seem good to me at the time, but he was good nonetheless.

The question that haunts our minds and burns us up with fear, doubt, and shame is not just a question of whether God is good but whether we're safe. We ask ourselves, *If God doesn't do this for me, will I be okay?* Most of us aren't walking out our faith like entitled trust-fund babies, demanding unreasonable things from our daddy. Our requests are simply human. Held behind the tears of everything we ask of our Creator is the one question we're afraid to ask out loud, lest we sound faithless and self-interested: *Will I be okay?*

Many of us have been taught by our church culture or our families that we shouldn't even ask such a question. Our shame screams, "Who cares if you're okay? You don't need to be okay—you just need to have faith." We are quick to dismiss ourselves when we have the audacity to be human. How dare we desire to be safe? How dare we ask God if we're going to be okay?

We're terrified to look that question in the face and admit that we care about the answer. We're so used to the idea of dying to self that we take it further than God intended and reject our human responses and concerns. We try to convince ourselves that it doesn't matter if we're okay, as long as God is glorified. But either we aren't being totally honest or we're in denial about the mental and emotional turmoil that waits for us in the aftermath of "he didn't."

It isn't brave in the "he didn't." It isn't pretty. Anguish waits in the aftermath, and it's eager to devour us whole. Of course we want to know that we'll be okay. Especially when we've felt the torment of God's face being turned away from us. David wrote about this feeling in Psalm 13:1-3:

> How long, LORD? Will you forget me forever?
>   How long will you hide your face from me?
> How long must I wrestle with my thoughts
>   and day after day have sorrow in my heart?
>   How long will my enemy triumph over me?
>
> Look on me and answer, LORD my God.
>   Give light to my eyes, or I will sleep in death.

When it seems like God has withheld his kindness from us, the sorrow we experience makes death seem like a reasonable alternative. Separation from him makes us feel empty, and we long to fill that void, to close the gap between us. We think the solution is for God to show he loves us by giving us what we want. So we pray for signs. We pray for a blessing. *Just show me you care, God.*

The pinnacle of faith (if there even is such a thing) isn't being able to say, "Even if he doesn't, I'll still know that he is good." That's a good and beautiful root to have your faith grow from, but it isn't complete. Faith isn't just believing that God is good no matter what; it's believing that you will be okay, no matter what.

Daniel 3 tells the story of Hananiah, Mishael, and Azariah* and how they refused to worship the Babylonian god Nebuchadnezzar set up, even upon threat of death. When Nebuchadnezzar told them they'd be thrown in the fire if they didn't bow, they responded, "So be it. Our God will rescue us. But even if he doesn't, we still won't worship yours." They believed they would be safe, even in the fire. Even if they died.

> When you believe that you're loved by him and you're secure in that love, you won't assume he's retracted his affection when your circumstances beg to differ.

Faith is believing not only that God's character is good and unchanging, but that his love for you is too. When you're able to do that, you're able to detach the outcome of your circumstances from the way God feels about you and acts toward you. When you believe that you're loved by him and you're secure in that love, you won't assume he's retracted his affection when your circumstances beg to differ.

Believing that you're safe with Jesus, no matter your circum-

---

* These are the Hebrew names of Shadrach, Meshach, and Abednego. Nebuchadnezzar changed their names to Babylonian names in an attempt to force them to assimilate into Babylonian culture. In the same way we don't refer to Daniel by his Babylonian name, Belteshazzar, I think it's important that we honor these men by referring to them by their given Hebrew names.

stances, requires just as much faith, if not more, as believing he is unquestionably good. You can believe that God is good, but do you believe he cares about you? You can believe that he's good, but do you believe you're safe even if his goodness comes at the expense of your joy? Do you believe that his concern for you stops and ends with whatever will bring him glory?

For most of my life, I believed that God's attitude toward me was one of loving indifference. Sure, he loved me, but as far as caring about the details of my life, it just was what it was. God was an authoritarian leader—aware of my pain, but not concerned about me personally. I just needed to suck it up, do the pull-myself-up-by-the-bootstraps thing, and march on.

There was an ache inside of me, yearning to feel safe, but I couldn't put my finger on exactly what it was. I was alive. I had food. I had a roof over my head. What more could I possibly need? But I was spiritually famished, feeding myself with bricks of theology instead of allowing the Holy Spirit to nourish my mind and my body with the love of the Father. I believed that God was only concerned about me to the extent of my usefulness to his Kingdom, and I didn't even think to ask for anything else. I never would have admitted that I wanted his comfort.

There's a phrase that has become popular as mental health conversations have come to be less of a taboo subject: "It's okay to not be okay." Those words give people who are struggling permission to take off the mask, to stop pretending that all is well, and to accept where they are. It *is* okay to not be okay. But I'd add that it's okay to *want* to be okay. There's nothing wrong with wanting to be safe. There's nothing wrong with needing comfort. There's nothing wrong with wanting to be okay. It's just human.

There's a beautiful passage in Exodus that displays both the concern and protective nature of our Creator:

> The LORD said, "I have observed the misery of my people in Egypt, and have heard them crying out because of their oppressors. I know about their sufferings, and I have come down to rescue them from the power of the Egyptians and to bring them from that land to a good and spacious land, a land flowing with milk and honey."
> EXODUS 3:7-8, CSB

The way God cared for the Israelites is the way he cares for all of us. He isn't just aware of the things that plague us; he's also concerned about the way those things affect us. He has a rescue plan—not just to deliver us from evil, but to bring us to a place of rest and peace.

Your desire for peace and safety comes from a hardwired inner knowledge that this is possible. Whether he does or doesn't answer your prayer the way you hope, you're right to wonder if you'll be okay.

When we're facing terrible things, we don't know if we'll end up sitting in the ashes of what we've lost or rejoicing in the sunlight of a miracle. When we're waiting to see where our story ends up, we need to hold on to who God is, not to what we hope he'll do for us. We need to believe that he's good, yes, but also that he's good to *us*.

THE DISTORTION:
God is not concerned for my well-being.

THE SHIFT:
God actively shows that he cares for me,
that he's concerned for me, and
that I am safe with him.

5

Peach Iced Tea
and Other Ebenezers

*Whatever may be the tensions and the stresses of a particular
day, there is always lurking close at hand the trailing
beauty of forgotten joy or unremembered peace.*

HOWARD THURMAN

THERE WERE A FEW MOMENTS throughout my pregnancy that became solid anchors in the sinking ship of my life. Sometimes you don't know something is important until later, but these were things I *knew* were important, even as they were happening. God was gracious to comfort my heart and breathe hope into my lungs when our girls' lives were hanging in the balance.

The first anchor came when I was sitting in the waiting room at the maternal fetal medicine office, waiting for the ultrasound that changed everything. My cousin (the pot-stirring one—you remember her) texted me a picture of onesies our other cousin had sent to her house. They were a pair, meant for two babies to wear at the same time.

The first onesie said, "Sometimes when you ask for a miracle . . ." and the second one said, "God gives you two."

I texted her back a few crying emojis and said, "They're perfect. So sweet!"

In that moment, the only thought in my head was how sweet it was that my cousin had bought these for the babies. We'd had so much grief and tragedy in recent years, and this double blessing felt like a gift to all of us. We joked that my aunt, who had passed away a few years earlier, had been involved in the "Should Kristen have twins?" discussion somewhere beyond the veil.

The onesies were far from my mind when I walked into the ultrasound room, but when I went back through the waiting room hours later, I remembered them. *That felt like a promise*, I thought. Why would she have texted me minutes before I walked into a room that threatened to suck the hope out of the very marrow of my body? What made our cousin pick that specific phrasing for those onesies? *Miracle. Two.* I clenched tight.

The next anchor came during the scan. We were twenty or thirty minutes in when the baby on my left side, whom the tech referred to as Baby B, kicked my stomach so hard it knocked the wand out of the tech's hand and onto the bed beside me.

We laughed, and I passed the wand back to her. "Baby B is a feisty one, isn't she?"

I smiled. I knew she was. Her personality was so clear to me already. But to have someone else recognize the same thing felt really special.

As I watched Baby B kicking and making the tech's job harder than it needed to be, I thought, *That's Lydia.*

With our other kids, Zach and I hadn't been sure about their names until they were born. We'd narrow it down to one or two and then make the final decision after we met them. I've always thought there's something sweet about seeing your baby for the first time and connecting a name to this tiny little person. We were planning to do the same with our girls.

At this point, I was nineteen weeks pregnant, so we'd just begun tossing names back and forth. We'd known there were two babies for about four weeks, and we'd only known they were girls for a few days. The fact that we had any names in mind at all was a miracle in itself.

There were two we really loved: Chloe Rebecca and Lydia Joy—named after my sister and my sister-in-law and two New Testament church leaders. We were pretty sure those would be their names, but we didn't know who was who yet. We planned to wait until they were born and then decide who was Lydia and who was Chloe.

So naming Lydia first, during the scan that would determine her life unviable, was pretty wild. Almost as soon as the doctor delivered the bad news, I knew the Holy Spirit had spoken her name to me.

The last big anchor came the following day, in the form of a giant Old Navy package. It was sitting on the floor of my bedroom in my mother- and father-in-law's house. Zach's mom had gone through my registry and ordered just about everything on it. After the ultrasound, she let me know that the box was in the room but warned me not to open it if it would be too difficult.

I wondered what it would mean for me to open the package. Would it be a step of faith to unfold clothes meant for babies who might never wear them? Or would it be reckless, self-inflicted emotional abuse? Would I be traumatizing myself to prove a point?

Later that night, when I was alone, I opened the package and pulled the plastic off every outfit. A few pieces of clothing in, it hit me that there were *two* of each outfit.

This made sense, of course, but I hadn't registered for two of each item. I pulled up my list to make sure, but no. I'd obeyed the advice from all the twins in my life, who warned me about the embarrassment of being forced to wear matching outfits and begged me not to ruin my daughters' lives in that way.

So I carefully selected outfits that coordinated but didn't match, because I didn't want my daughters to grow up hating me! But there they were. Every single outfit I'd picked out was doubled. *Two. There are two. I'm going to have two babies.* It felt like a promise—like a giant deposit of hope directly from the heart of the Father.

My mother-in-law had no way of knowing that those doubled outfits would be an anchor for my hope, but they were. I had my miracle onesies and a pile of doubled Old Navy outfits as tangible hope that things would be okay.

Over the next few months, whenever things looked bleak, I would close my eyes and return to the floor of that room in my in-laws' house. I'd remember what it felt like to open the packages while I fought fatalistic thoughts like *I'm so glad I didn't buy matching outfits. At least if one of them survives, I won't have to toss all the matches we won't need.* And then having those thoughts interrupted with hope as every outfit had a double. It was an intoxicating kind of hope. It felt rebellious. Did I truly dare to hope right now? How audacious.

When our hearts are broken, the things that comfort us aren't theological discoveries or doctrinal truths. The strongest anchors are moments in our lives when God intervenes in sacred and specific ways. The times God is tangibly faithful and obviously present remind us that he has come through for us before, and they give us hope that he'll do it again.

The book of 1 Samuel recounts a story about a battle won by the Israelites that was, logistically speaking, impossible for them to win. The Philistine army was bigger and stronger, and yet, to the surprise of all parties involved, the Israelites were victorious.

To honor the victory the Lord had given them, Samuel took a stone and turned it upright. He named it *Ebenezer*, which means "stone of help." The stone would serve to remind them that "the LORD has helped us to this point."* This was not an altar of worship but a point of reference. It was a way of telling the Israelites, "Hey, let's not forget what God did for us here. This is how we'll remember." It was a physical reminder of a supernatural provision and intervention.

The darkness of suffering, heartache, and trauma casts wide shadows over the good things in our lives. The enemy takes advantage of our weakened spirits and whispers convincing lies about who we are and who God is. He loves to try to break the image of God in us. The first lie that entered the atmosphere of the perfect world God created was that God wasn't telling the truth.

The pesky snake that ruined everything slithered up to Eve and whispered a lie that we are all familiar with: "Did God *really* say that?" He planted doubt in Eve about who God is and fractured the image of God in her heart.

When our image of God is fractured, we make decisions that reflect the image we see. Eve believed the snake. He told her that she wouldn't die and that God was holding out on her in an attempt to stop her from being like him. She believed him, so she ate the fruit and hid from God. She thought that being filled with knowledge and understanding would make her like God, but instead it made her ashamed. She knew it wasn't God who had betrayed her but she who had betrayed God.

When you're in crisis, your heart feels fragile. That sneaky little lie, "Is God *really* who he said he is?" is the crack to the glass. The

---

* *1 Samuel 7:12*, CSB

enemy will use your circumstances to convince you that God is not who he said he is and that you can be more than he said you can be.

And you know, sometimes the lies feel good. When you're going through something brutal, it feels better to think that God is a jerk than to believe that he's still good. At least if he's a jerk, the pain makes sense.

This lie is easier to believe when our trust in God is broken. Its shadow will creep over every good and beautiful thing that has come into your life and will turn every flower into a useless weed. It will twist the truth and deceive you and fill your mind with poison.

But we don't have to let our circumstances rewrite our history. This is when we have to remember the times God came through for us in the past. When we don't, it's all too easy to allow lies to create an image of God that isn't real.

I spent about a year of my life struggling with panic attacks, massive depressive episodes, and dark, intrusive thoughts that led to a slight suicide ideation. It unhinged my life. My marriage almost fell apart. I spent more time than I'd ever willingly admit in the emergency room, trying to persuade doctors and nurses to take me seriously because I was obviously dying.

My mental health crisis wasn't just a wrecking ball to my life and relationships but to my body as well. I started experiencing night terrors, sleep paralysis, and chronic pain in my back, stomach, and chest. My anxiety and depression metabolized in my body, and I suffered physically in a way that left me exhausted, weak, and incapable of performing some of the most basic tasks.

Eventually, with time and therapy, I started to heal. I made some major changes in the ways I was taking care of myself. I learned to say yes to the right things and no to the things that weren't right for me. I made a list of things that were causing me stress and triggering my anxiety, and I crossed off as many as I could. Zach and I threw a fortress over our family and committed to make healing my brain our number-one focus. Zach and I had honest, brutal conversations that helped us really see and understand each other, and we healed our relationship. When I think back on that time now, I feel absolutely zero awkwardness about saying that I'm a survivor.

I survived. I didn't want to. But I did. It was brutal in ways that are hard to explain unless you know the pain that mental illness can unleash in your life.

But let me tell you something about lies. In the middle of a crisis, they feel familiar and even comforting. When we were in the middle of spiritual abuse and a total expulsion from our faith community, I crawled into bed with depression and anxiety. I welcomed them back like old friends. I wasn't afraid of them. I knew them—I knew what to expect from them. I knew the hallways that would lead me to the rooms of my mind where darkness was waiting to swallow me, and I opened every door. The accusatory thoughts, the fatalistic conclusions, the worst-case scenarios, the urge to rip off all my clothes and start running and never stop—they were all a comfort to me.

What was happening with our church was so relationally and emotionally traumatic that I really believed it would be easier to hide in the darkness than to face what was happening. I traded what didn't make sense for what was familiar. I didn't care about the consequences for putting out a welcome mat for those emotions. I wanted nothing more than to be swallowed whole.

I was more than willing to trade this raw, unbearable pain for a pain I knew—a pain I could handle, a pain I could live with. The pain was so consuming that I would have traded it for my own internal suffering in half a second. If God had handed both to me on a platter and said, "Pick your poison," I'd have chosen the poison I'd already tasted. Every single time. I would have happily chosen the poison I knew I could survive.

But we don't get to pick our poison, no matter how enticing the lie is that it's the better choice. Sometimes darkness feels safer than the light, because in the light we have to face the truth—and the truth is often the more terrifying option. In the light, we have to come to terms with the reality of our pain and the truth of who God is. When facing the truth means facing the parts of God's character that don't line up perfectly with who we believed him to be, we hide. Like Adam and Eve hid from God in the bushes so he wouldn't see their nakedness, we hide from God so we won't see who he really is. We hide from him in our pain because we don't trust him to still be good in spite of it.

Our crisis with Chloe and Lydia gave me the opportunity to put to the test what I'd learned as we walked through the pain of our church situation. I had to decide if I was going to hide or if I was going to stand in the light and see our reality for what it was. Would I choose to stay in the shadows that kept truth hidden, or would I stand out in the open and boldly face God?

When we hide, we rob ourselves of the opportunity to remember. Throughout the story of God and his people, he often warned them not to forget. In Psalm 78, we're urged to remember God's faithfulness and to tell our children about it: "He commanded our ancestors to teach to their children so that a future generation— children yet to be born—might know. They were to rise and tell their children so that they might put their confidence in God and not forget God's works, but keep his commands."* There's a

---

* *Psalm 78:5-7,* CSB

reason Moses told the Israelites to remember the day they were rescued from Egypt.* There's a reason God said to "remember what happened long ago."† The pattern is repeated throughout Scripture: *Remember; don't forget. Remember; don't forget.*

When we forget what God has done for us, we forget who God is. A good example of this is found in Psalm 77. In the first part of the passage, the writer is distressed: "I refused to be comforted. I think of God; I groan; I meditate; my spirit becomes weak." Then the psalmist begins to ask questions: "Will the Lord reject forever and never again show favor? Has his faithful love ceased forever? Is his promise at an end for all generations?" His questions lead him to the conclusion that God has changed: "I am grieved that the right hand of the Most High has changed."

But when he gets to the end of his lament, he calls himself back and says, "I will remember the Lord's works. . . . I will reflect on all you have done and meditate on your actions." He remembers who God is: "God, your way is holy. What god is great like God? You are the God who works wonders."‡

When we are disoriented by pain, our vision blurs and we start to see God through the lens of our circumstances. Our image of him becomes distorted. Looking back to a time when he was faithful can be painful. It can make you feel like the writer of that psalm—like God's favor has run out. His love has hit its peak, and now he has rejected you and abandoned you, and he is ambivalent toward your hurt.

But God's character doesn't change. His love doesn't alter. He can't be moved. We mark his faithfulness not to pour salt in our wounds but to stir hope in our spirits again.

※

---

* *Exodus 13:3*
† *Isaiah 46:9,* CSB
‡ *Psalm 77,* CSB

When I look back over my life, one of the most painful—but also significant—ebenezers came when Zach and I decided to leave our church. The decision was ours to make, but in reality, our hand was forced.

Zach was sort of a jack-of-all-trades pastor on staff. His main title was youth pastor, but he also led worship and filled in the gaps wherever he was needed, especially during a pastoral transition that started about six months after we arrived. After the pastor who hired Zach retired, a new pastor came to the church, and there were red flags right away. But we loved our church family, we loved our home, and we felt strongly that God had brought us to this church and this city. So we tried to compromise, to make it work. We made excuses for the pastor, and we prayed and prayed and prayed that we wouldn't have to leave. But it quickly became clear to us that this wasn't going to be sustainable for our family.

The pastor's leadership style was authoritarian, and he began crossing lines into controlling aspects of our private lives that were inappropriate and, frankly, unbiblical. Once we made it clear to the pastor (and the pastor only) that serious boundaries had been crossed, we made the decision to leave quickly and quietly.

When we confronted the pastor (as Matthew 5 encourages us to do), his response was to unleash on us the reality of what had been happening behind the scenes, without our knowledge. He informed us that for the past several months, he and the board and their spouses had been having meetings behind closed doors. In those meetings, it was decided that Zach and I were unfit to minister. The pastor had collected and presented what he called "evidences" to discredit us and disqualify us from pastoral ministry. *"Everyone* agrees with me," he told my husband.

According to what the pastor shared with us, we hadn't done anything *wrong*, except for being bad parents to one of our children. (He made a point of saying that the other two were just fine.) This wasn't sin, he assured us. It wasn't that we weren't a fit for the church. But the pastor and the board had decided we weren't reaching a bar they expected us to reach, without telling us where the bar was, that we hadn't been reaching it, or what we could do to better meet those expectations.

Years later, one of the board members who was involved apologized to us, describing those meetings as a witch hunt, bent on catching us, accusing us, and proving our inadequacy as both ministers and parents.

People we had known for decades had, in what felt like an instant, decided we were no longer worthy of respect or kindness. One Sunday I went to greet a friend as I normally would, with a hug, and she narrowed her eyes, turned her back to me, and walked away. Later that week, words that Zach had spoken to the pastor in confidence came back to me in twisted, manipulated ways. Words he'd said had been removed from their context to make him look terrible. I watched people I loved duck behind displays in grocery stores and powerwalk across parking lots to avoid talking to me. I didn't understand. I didn't know the story they'd been told. I hadn't been allowed to share mine. We didn't know who to trust, and it was so lonely. We chose to leave, but we really had no choice. We were being pushed out.

We were so hurt and blindsided that we didn't trust our perception of what was happening. We called some of our old college professors, mentors in other states, family members who were pastors, and friends serving in similar positions at other churches. We even reached out to ministerial professionals. We didn't want to leave. We wanted someone to tell us we were overreacting—that we should get back to work, get over it, and make the necessary changes so we could stay.

Out of the dozens of wise counselors we sought, not one person said we were in the wrong. They all said the same thing: "Run as fast as you can."

But it didn't make sense. We'd done all the right things. We'd followed the biblical model for addressing conflict. We'd followed the rules. So why was this happening? What had we done wrong?

I replayed every conversation, every look, every shoulder brush to try to pinpoint the moment I'd screwed up and ruined our careers and ministries. I drove myself crazy trying to find a reason so I could find a solution. My formula wasn't adding up. We were supposed to grow old here. God had brought us here. He had spoken so clearly. And now it was all falling apart around us, and I had no idea why. What had we done to deserve this?

How could we decide what to do next when we had one hundred dollars in our bank account and we had one week from our final Sunday to leave our house (which was part of our pay package)? How was I supposed to function when my husband was so broken he hadn't moved from the couch in three days?

We had no job prospects, no severance, no help at all. How could we process our pain when we weren't allowed to tell the truth about what had happened? How could we seek the Lord's will when we'd thought we'd been in it already? I didn't even know what it meant to be "in the Lord's will" anymore.

❋

Ebenezer stones return us to the joy of our salvation and help us remember the truth of God's love and character. When our pain gives a megaphone to the lies that say, *See? See how God has failed you!* our ebenezers stand in front of us, reminding us where we once stood and what God did there. The lies can shout as loud as they want, but rock doesn't shake easily.

Do you want to know my silliest ebenezer stone? It's a peach iced tea that was sitting in a fridge in a bodega on Frederick Douglass Boulevard in Harlem, New York City.

When we left our church, we had nowhere to go. With no jobs and no housing, we moved into my parents' apartment in New York City. As time passed, my mourning over what we lost at our church turned into anger. That anger turned into desperation.

I was desperate to hear from God. I was lonely and isolated. I felt forgotten by everyone I knew, especially the God I thought would never leave me or forsake me. But there I was in the South Bronx, feeling every shade of forsaken. I begged God to show me that he loved me and cared about me.

I have this specific peach tea from a specific brand that I've been drinking for almost my entire adult life, but when we moved to New York City, I wasn't able to find it anywhere. I was without my emotional vice when I desperately needed it, and if God would just send me one, I'd know he loved me.

Of course it was silly. Of course it was desperate. But when hope is on short supply, you'll reach for anything. I was dislocating my shoulder for this reach, but I didn't care. Just as I was giving up hope and accepting that God had abandoned me forever, I threw one last prayer to the wind. *Please let it be in this store. Then I'll know you love me.*

As I turned into the bodega, it was as if a spotlight from heaven shone down on the refrigerator. There, sitting on the shelf, was one ice-cold peach tea. It was waiting for me, as if it knew I was coming—the only peach tea in all of New York City.

Sure, it was no parting of the Red Sea. But it was just as miraculous to me. Up until that moment, I'd felt like God was ambivalent and distant. A tea in a random grocery store in Harlem was like writing on the wall of my weary heart. It was a celebration, a connection point between my Creator and me. And now that reminder of God's tenderness still anchors me, holding me steady when life knocks me around. I think about it when I'm sad and struggling and wondering if he sees me and cares about me. I think back to that day and remember how alone I felt when I asked God for a simple thing, and how he gave it to me. A peach tea Ebenezer stone.

Of course, God doesn't always respond in the way we ask or the way we think he will. Often the ebenezers of our lives are moments of unexpected goodness and joy. A victory where we expected loss. Joy when we thought we'd be sad indefinitely. Ebenezers, in themselves, aren't signs that we've asked for but moments that mark the recognizable goodness and favor of God.

When we mark these moments of God's faithfulness, we help our hearts return to joy. When joy fades from our hearts, our pain becomes louder and more acute. But when we return to joy, we remind our hearts and our minds and our bodies of the joy we can have, at all times, because of Christ.

Ebenezers are ordinary reminders of when God did extraordinary things for us.

The ebenezers in our lives are stationary reminders, but when we remember them, we don't stay still. We move toward hope. We step into joy. We respond to what's true. *If God was faithful then, he is faithful now. And if he's faithful now, he'll be faithful in the future too.*

Our stones of remembrance show us that we don't have to be strong, because he is. We don't have to have all the answers, because he does. We don't need to know how it all turns out, because he's with us. That was enough then, and it's enough now. Ebenezers are ordinary reminders of when God did extraordinary things for us.

The roller coaster of our crisis pregnancy had me full of hope in one moment, certain everything would be okay because we had a good scan that day, and then crashing to the ground the next day with a bad one. It was emotional whiplash, being tossed between good news and bad news. Eventually, I ran out of room to feel anything at all.

In those moments of emotional exhaustion and numbness, I needed my ebenezers. I needed to remember the two sets of clothes. I needed to remember Lydia's name. I needed to remember every moment that shouted and whispered, *Remember what he did then? Remember who he is?* I'd go back to those memories again and again. I'd remind myself of them, and then I'd turn my face to God and beg him to remember too.

When I'm overwhelmed, I run. I quit projects. I don't respond to text messages. I cancel plans. We weren't created for pain; we were created for glory, so it's our natural response to do everything we can to avoid what will hurt us. We'll do anything to feel like we have control when things are spiraling out of our grasp.

I tend to get impulsive and have to actively fight the urge to tattoo my neck or pierce something. The way I bring myself to center and protect my body from becoming a victim to my cathartic lack of impulse control is to follow the map I made to my ebenezers.

I have journal pages dedicated to keeping track. I follow them like stepping stones, and they lead me straight to the Eden in my heart, when I believed God was good and kind.

At first, I started recording old moments of God's faithfulness. Some of them weren't even mine but things God had done for my parents or other people I loved. The thing is, when you start to question if God is good, you start to wonder if he has ever been good, to anyone. But when you think about the times he was good to other people, you start to remember the times he was good to you too.

The stones we set out to remember God's faithfulness aren't intended to mark times we escaped our pain, but the times God has shown himself to us in the middle of it. He might not have stopped the injury, but he showed that he was present, that he cares, and that he is faithful to his kids. We mark the stones with blood and tears. When we visit them, we remember both what they cost us and what God did for us there.

You'd think it would be easier to remember how big and powerful God is. You'd think that if we have even one moment to mark down and remember, that should be enough to change us forever. In the heat of a victory, you might even convince yourself that you'll never forget what God did in that moment. But as time goes on, we forget. Unless we have a map.

We don't really know which moments will end up having the most impact on our spiritual lives, but God does. And I think he speaks to each of us in the language we understand. He sees our aches, and he knows the cure. Sometimes the moments that end up being the most significant are the times not a single soul other than you would find significant. I have seen the goodness of the Lord in the land of the living, and I've experienced his goodness in the valley of the shadow of death, and yet what I'm telling you about is that peach tea—that silly little peach tea.

But I marked that moment. I felt loved, seen, and cared for by the God I'd been convinced wasn't who he said he was. Ebenezer stones hold us accountable to the truth as we lived it. It doesn't matter even if it *is* coincidence or luck. All that matters is that God used it to breathe hope into my broken heart. Our ebenezers anchor us to the heart of God, reminding us that he is good, he is kind, and he is faithful, even when everything around us is screaming that he isn't.

The darkness tries to hide the light. It masquerades as truth and tries to distort what is good. It tries to make you forget. It tells tempting lies and cloaks them with familiarity. But in those moments when suffering tries to make you forget, your ebenezers invite you to remember.

We go back to the Garden and hear the snake whisper, "Did God really say that?" And we start to think that maybe God didn't. We can go back to our ebenezers and dismiss them too. *Did God really put that tea in the fridge or was it just a grocery store employee? Did God really whisper Lydia's name or was it just that you had a 50/50 chance of naming the baby that was sick and it happened to be her?*

Remembering who God is changes the way you interact with him in your pain. When you remember that God will be faithful again because he has been faithful before, it changes your response to your circumstances. You're able to engage with confidence—not because of your own strength, but because of the God who is carrying you. Your prayers might still be desperate, but there's a thread of belief that ties your heart to heaven. You trust that he hears you and has his face turned toward you, not away from you.

Even in your darkest, weakest moments, you can remember his goodness. It doesn't always feel safe to follow that map to your stones. But turning your face toward the past gives you a much-needed reprieve from the present.

Our ebenezers give us permission to detach from the weight of our current burdens so we can attach ourselves to the weight of God's glory. We can think back on those moments when we weren't sure he'd come through at all. But he did. And it was good. And you were okay.

> *Your prayers might still be desperate, but there's a thread of belief that ties your heart to heaven. You trust that he hears you and has his face turned toward you, not away from you.*

THE DISTORTION:
When I suffer,
God has abandoned me.

❋

THE SHIFT:
When my pain makes me feel like
God has forgotten me, I can remember the
times he's been faithful to me in the past and
trust that he'll be faithful to me again.

6

Deep Cries to Deep

The house of my soul is too small for you to come to it.

May it be enlarged by you. It is in ruins: restore it.

AUGUSTINE

THROUGHOUT THE REST OF MY PREGNANCY, I made lists of practical prayer requests and sent them out via text messages and social media posts:

- Pray that Baby B's blood flow is normal at the next scan.
- Pray that our insurance will cover the next appointment.
- Pray that both babies will continue to grow at a survivable rate.

I'd never really been a "prayer request" kind of girl. I was more of the "raise your hand if you have an unspoken request" kind. I'd had experience leading corporate prayer, and I could fashion words to pray over someone at the altar, but praying for myself—and asking for prayer for my family and me—was a challenge.

When I was a girl, I'd lay in my bed at night listing the sins I'd committed that day, one by one, and asking God to forgive me. "Please forgive me for calling Christopher stupid. Please forgive me for lying about how many bites of spaghetti I took. Please forgive me for being mad." My mind couldn't rest until I knew that if I died in my sleep or if a car ran through my room or if an asteroid fell on our house, I'd wake up in heaven.

These days we call those kinds of thoughts "intrusive," but back then, I saw them as my safeguards against hearing the words "Depart from me; I never knew you."

One of my earliest memories is asking my Sunday school teacher, "If I told a lie and then got hit by a car and died, would I go to hell?" She told me, emphatically, that I would. Well, I wasn't going to let *that* happen. I'd make sure no sin was left unconfessed.

That's how I learned that God was only concerned about my holiness, and the only time he was interested in a conversation with me was when I was apologizing for all the things I'd done wrong. So that's how I prayed.

I prayed for my friends, for missionaries, for sick people I knew, and maybe for a new toy or something, and then I'd list every sin I could think of. I'd end each prayer time with, "Please forgive me for any sins I forgot about. I'm sorry for those too."

Not that this habit did anything to calm my anxiety about hell. I was constantly terrified that I was forgetting something and that a sneaky little sin would cost me my eternity and private mansion in heaven.*

The actual problem was that I thought prayer was transactional. Conversations with God were for a purpose: forgiveness, healing, or to get something I really wanted. I didn't have a framework for simply talking to Jesus.

---

* Arguably, praying off every sin before I fell asleep was better than praying to the devil, which I also did, but only once and just so he'd make me sick enough to stay home from school!

I think it's interesting that a lot of us who came to faith in the evangelical tradition are taught that following Jesus is about having a personal relationship with him, but the way we're taught to pray and to interact with him isn't relational at all.

If I have a relationship with Jesus, why do I have to be so careful about what I say to him? If I have a relationship with Jesus, why do I have to fear that every mistake will send me to hell? If I have a relationship with Jesus, why does it feel so unsafe sometimes?

We talk about relationship without defining what that actually means. We assume that a friend is someone who automatically takes our side, who always sees things the way we do. We apply our human-to-human relationship dynamics to our human-to-more-than-human relationship with Christ, and then we're surprised when it doesn't work out the way we think it should. We take the Bible's "friend of God" descriptor and think it means that God will give us what we want, because that's what friends do, right? We take our ideas of what friendship means and fashion them into an image that reflects those friendship ideals. We expect God to move and act like us instead of being the God who is sovereign and all-powerful.

Sometimes words like *all-powerful* and *sovereign* cause a disconnect in our hearts between us and God. If God is all those big, powerful things, then why would he care about me? When we hear *sovereign*, we think *distant*. When we think *all-powerful*, we feel small and inconsequential. We want a sovereign, all-powerful God when we ask for big things, but we don't like to think of him that way when we need him to be our friend.

Nichole Nordeman has a beautiful song called "Small Enough," where she calls out to "the God of ancient mysteries whose every sign and wonder turn the pages of our history." She goes on to say that her heart is heavy: "I cannot keep from whispering this prayer,

'Are you there?'" She beautifully captures the tension of how a God who is big and powerful can still meet us in our quiet moments.

Sometimes our idea of what it means for God to be our friend and what it means for him to be sovereign can prevent us from approaching him in prayer. But we can trust him to be both friend and sovereign God.

❋

Prayer is at once simple and complex. A child can do it, and yet the most brilliant mind can't get to the depths of it in a lifetime.

Some of us learned to pray by watching what was modeled in our churches and by our spiritual mentors. Some of us learned to pray by reading, memorizing, and reciting liturgical prayers. Some of us learned to pray simply by talking to Jesus.

Tim Keller wrote a whole book on prayer, and even with all his education, experience, and decades of pursuing Christ, said, "Prayer is nonetheless an exceedingly difficult subject to write about. That is not primarily because it is so indefinable but because, before it, we feel so small and helpless."[1] What a strange concept prayer is, when you really think about it. We can talk to *God*? In our *minds*? Weird.

I'm not the first person to struggle with prayer and to wrestle with the idea of prayer in the first place. In *Confessions*, Augustine asks, "How shall I call upon my God, my God and Lord? Surely when I call on him, I am calling on him to come into me. But what place is there in me where my God can enter into me? 'God made heaven and earth' (Gen. 1:1). Where may he come to me? Lord my God, is there any room in me which can contain you?"[2]

In an attempt to resolve the mystery surrounding prayer, some people try to turn it into a formula. We're taught to pray in a way that moves God toward action. We quote Scriptures like Psalm 37:4: "He will give you the desires of your heart" and Matthew 21:22: "Whatever you ask in prayer, you will receive, if you have faith" (ESV). We hold those words tightly and think that we're entitled to receive whatever it is we're asking of him. We're encouraged to "press in," have more faith, and not to leave the altar until we get what we came for.

We call for him to come to us, like Augustine said. But what's the difference between praying in faith and praying to bend God's neck to our will? When does praying boldly become an unwillingness to accept anything other than our own plans? A. W. Tozer says, "We want nothing radical or out of the ordinary, and we want God to accommodate us at our convenience. Thus we attach a rider to every prayer, making it impossible for God to answer it."[3]

Our prayers become little more than a list of demands when we put our own conditions on each request. You know and I know that we can't actually tie the hands of God, but when we pray for a specific thing to be given to us in a specific way, we make it pretty impossible to recognize when God has answered our prayer.

I think a lot of us probably ask ourselves, especially in the middle of crisis, what the point of prayer is. If God is sovereign and knows everything that will happen and *controls* everything that will happen, can our prayers actually change his mind? Can our will for our own lives become aligned to his if we pray hard enough? These are valid questions, and there aren't really easy answers for them. God's Word is full of things that seem to stand in juxtaposition with each other, which can make understanding something abstract like prayer a lot more difficult.

Scripture tells us that he doesn't change his mind. According to 1 Samuel 15:29, "He is not a man, that He would change His mind" (NASB). Isaiah 31:2 says he "does not retract His words" (NASB). But then we see story after story where he seems to do just that! In Jeremiah 26:19, God changes his mind about sending the disaster he'd pronounced against his people. Exodus 32:14 says, "The Lord changed his mind about the harm which he said he would do" (NASB). In Amos 7:3 we read, "The Lord changed his mind about this" (NASB). So which is it? Is God's mind made up, or can we make him bend?

When I was seventeen, I had my first serious boyfriend. He was five years older, and he was the first boy I'd ever dated. I wanted to marry him immediately.

I imagined us getting engaged within the year, married soon after, setting up a home together, serving in ministry together—the whole dream. I wanted this so badly that I started looking for signs and confirmations everywhere. At the time, I didn't know how to pray. I didn't know how to listen to the voice of God. I didn't know what the Holy Spirit sounded like.

Since I didn't know how to discern God's voice from my own, I tried throwing out fleeces anywhere I thought they'd land.* I'd close my eyes and flip through my Bible, and when I landed on a verse with my boyfriend's name, I knew it was the Lord telling me to marry him. I'd look at the Florida sky and say, "If it rains today for seven minutes, that's God confirming that this relationship is okay."† I even called my mom once to tell her, "Guess what? God told me I was going to marry him!"

I was never so sure of what I wanted and so unsure of what God had for me. I told myself I wanted to be in the will of God, but my prayers were not for his will to be done but for him to confirm that his will was aligned with mine.

---

* "Throwing out a fleece" is a phrase that essentially means "testing God." It comes from the story of Gideon in Judges 6. Gideon wanted to be sure he was really hearing the voice of God, so he laid out a piece of wool overnight and told God that if this message was really from him, he'd confirm it by letting the wool get wet while the ground around the wool stayed dry. Testing God in this way isn't a bad or sinful thing. God was gracious to Gideon and did what he asked. But as we grow in our faith, we learn to hear God's voice and respond to it and won't need a fleece anymore.
† Since the average length of a Florida rain is five to seven minutes, this was a very strategic and convenient fleece.

It took two years for me to start questioning if this was the right guy for me. I was terrified to break up with him. I wasn't even nineteen years old, but somehow I thought my eligibility window was gone. After my relationship with him, I'd be single forever—I just knew it.

In my mind, I had only two options: marry this guy I was maturing out of or break up with him and (best-case scenario) be a single missionary for the rest of my life. I decided to lay my options before the Lord and toss the dice, so to speak.

I sat on my bedroom floor at my parents' house, lit a candle, opened my Bible and my journal, and just sat. I didn't pray. I didn't speak. I just waited.

A friend had told me that when my mind was saying something my heart had a hard time accepting, it might be the voice of the Lord. And that's what happened.

I listened, and as I stayed quiet, I couldn't ignore the pressing sense that I needed to break up with him. The thought terrified me. I honestly, with my whole heart, believed that breaking up with him meant deciding to be single forever. I would never be a wife. I would never be a mother.

But I made that phone call anyway, because I believed God told me to. And when I did, I felt free. For the first time in my life, I had successfully had a conversation with God.

As I grew in my faith, I learned to discern the voice of the Holy Spirit from every other voice, including my own. My prayers grew from "Please forgive me for my sins" and "Please give me what I want" to "Show me what you want for me." But even as I grew in my faith, the only way I knew how to pray was with myself at the center of it. What God had for *me*. What God was trying to show *me*. What God wanted from *me*. Me. Me. Me.

It wasn't that I was uniquely narcissistic or self-centered, I just didn't know any other way to pray. I didn't know any other way to follow Jesus. I'd been taught that he was my personal Savior, that he was thinking about me when he died, and that it was my sin that had put him there in the first place. I'd been taught that he had a plan for my life, that he would give me the desires of my heart, that he wanted a personal relationship with me, and that I was special, his favorite. These things weren't wrong or harmful in themselves, but they perpetuated a type of self-serving faith that subtly grew into spiritual entitlement. He was *my* Savior. He owed me.

Self-focused spirituality is dry. We pray for ourselves because that's all that's ever been at stake for us. We pray the way we think God wants us to pray, assuming that if we line up the words just right, he'll listen and we'll receive. When things are going well in our lives and the transactional nature of our prayers is working in our favor, we rarely feel the need for anything to change. Our prayers don't go deeper, because they don't have to. We don't even know what lies beyond the surface of our faith because we haven't had to look there yet.

But when something terrible takes a shovel to the soil of your faith, you find out what's growing below the surface. Your beliefs about prayer disintegrate somewhere past the first shovel dig. When you don't have the framework to form a prayer that will reach through your pain and all you can do is groan, that's where you'll find how far the roots of your faith have stretched.

※

I've never been in the radius of a bomb blast before, but I think trauma is kind of like that. Your ears start ringing, your vision gets blurry, the world begins to spin, and you lose your footing. Everyone outside the blast keeps moving as if nothing happened while you're trying to figure out how to stand on your feet—if you even have feet anymore.

The day we were given the news that our daughters' lives were likely not viable while I was sitting on that crinkly hospital paper, holding my phone instead of my husband's hand, the words that I choked out, "Oh my God," became some of the only words I could form in God's direction for a while. After that, there were only groans.

I didn't pray for our daughters. At least, not in the way anyone expected I would pray (or the way they would pray if they were in my shoes) or the way I'd been taught. My mom's dad, my Papa, was an old Southern Pentecostal preacher, and when he prayed, his whole body was included in the process. He paced, he cried, he moaned, he quoted Scripture.

One time he prayed for me by sitting on the floor next to me, wrapping his arms around my legs and crying out to God for my soul. I've never prayed like that in my life. In fact, in college, Zach and I were criticized by school leadership because of our lack of emoting and hand raising in prayer and worship. It just isn't my personality to pray that way, but if there were ever a time to pray like a Pentecostal, this was it. But I didn't.

During my pregnancy with the girls, I would sit on my bed and in my car and in the doctor's office, trying to form words to pray. I'm a pastor's kid, a Bible school graduate, a former ministry leader—*I know how to pray*. I imagined the words in my head. I saw myself saying them. I could form the perfectly crafted, melodic, poetic, heartfelt lines with ease. But the thought of saying them out loud made my stomach churn. They weren't enough.

Whatever words I came up with, they would be empty and flat. No matter how beautiful or biblical they were, they wouldn't capture what my soul was feeling. How could God be moved by words that didn't even break the skin of what I was experiencing?

I was in absolute anguish. My soul was in torment. I was helpless, out of control, heartbroken, and petrified. Any words other than a whispered "Please" felt like empty platitudes—disrespectful to the sacred crisis I was in.

I was slogging through mud and begging God to be with me, but my words weren't enough. I didn't want to crowd the space between God and me with silly things like words. I wanted a clear path, with nothing between us besides the miracle I was hoping for.

What do you say when you're standing in front of the throne of God, completely out of words? You are speechless, not because you're so in awe of your Creator, but because you're so defeated you can't form a coherent thought, much less speak one. You can't ask. You can't yell. You can't accuse. You can't beg.

How can you speak when you can barely breathe? What if you crawl to the feet of Jesus but can't manage to lift your head to speak to him?

Some theologies teach that Jesus won't turn his face toward you unless you approach him boldly, loudly, with confidence, and with unshaken faith—as if we can impress him with our bravery.

I didn't feel brave. I've never felt brave in my life. And I believe that God is much kinder than that.

Remember the woman in Jesus' time who had been bleeding for twelve years? She spent everything she had trying to get answers from different doctors, but her condition continued to get worse. In those days, female bleeding was considered unclean. Anything a woman touched while on her period would become impure. Sex was prohibited, as was entering the Temple.*

Try to imagine, first of all, being on your period for twelve years. Yikes. Now imagine having to live as an outcast, unclean,

---

*This Jewish practice, called Niddah, is derived from Leviticus 15, which gives purification rituals for female bleeding.

not allowed to touch or be touched. This woman was undoubt-
edly defeated and exhausted. Twelve years of isolation, rejection,
questions, seeking answers, and spending everything, only to
get a medical diagnosis of "There's nothing we can do." She was
desperate.

But then she heard about Jesus. He had been stirring up all
kinds of talk as he hopped from town to town healing people,
casting out demons, and feeding large crowds with a few loaves
and a couple of fish. He was her last resort.

One day a crowd formed around Jesus as he was walking
through this woman's city. She thought, *If I can just touch the
hem of his robe, I'll be healed.* And that's exactly what happened.
Immediately after brushing her fingers across his robe, her bleeding stopped and she was well.

When Jesus felt the power leave his body, he turned around
and asked, "Who touched me?"

His disciples said, "There are all kinds of people touching
you—look around!"

But Jesus knew this touch was different. He locked eyes with
the woman, and she was terrified. Of course she would be! She'd
just touched *Jesus* while on her period. A huge, punishable no-no.

But Jesus didn't scold her—he honored her. "Your faith has
made you well," he told her. "Go in peace and be healed of your
disease."

The Gospel writers deemed this story so important to Jesus'
ministry that three out of four of them included it in their
account.[*] This act of healing is arguably one of Jesus' most radical moments as Messiah. He healed a woman who touched him
without permission—an act that should have made him impure.
Not only did he heal her, but he did so without even being asked.

Matthew 9:20-22; Mark 5:24-34; Luke 8:43-48

How countercultural of him. And how audacious of her to crawl through the crowd, risking her own neck to touch the hem of his clothing—all in the hope that enough power would reach her fingertips to give her relief. She didn't ask. She didn't beg. She just touched him.

This woman wasn't the only one Jesus healed without being asked. He singled out a blind man and healed him.* He healed a paralyzed man at the pool of Bethsaida, and the guy didn't even know Jesus was the one who did it until later!† Jesus cast out demons without any expression of faith from the person they were tormenting.‡

Jesus doesn't need our words to meet our needs.

When Peter sliced off the ear of the Roman soldier, Jesus picked it up and put it back on before the soldier had time to register what had happened.§

Jesus doesn't need our words to meet our needs. We don't have to wax poetic in our prayers to bend his ear. He doesn't require our pithy words or clever negotiations. We don't need to prove anything to him or persist until he relents. Sometimes he invites our faith. Sometimes he invites our asks. But sometimes all he wants is our reach.

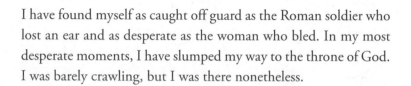

I have found myself as caught off guard as the Roman soldier who lost an ear and as desperate as the woman who bled. In my most desperate moments, I have slumped my way to the throne of God. I was barely crawling, but I was there nonetheless.

---

* *John 9*
† *John 5:1-15*
‡ *Luke 8:26-39*
§ *John 18:10; Luke 22:51*

There is comfort at the feet of Jesus even when there aren't answers. When words fail us and our hearts are broken and the ringing in our ears is so loud we can't think—when we don't even have the strength to stretch out a hand to touch the hem of his clothes—our spirits groan for us.

Psalm 42:7 describes this experience beautifully: "Deep calls to deep in the roar of your waterfalls; all your breakers and your billows have swept over me" (csb). The writer is so overwhelmed by darkness and despair that it feels like being caught in a powerful undertow—like being hit with wave after wave, getting pulled farther from shore and deeper underwater until you lose all sense of direction.

In the deepest parts of your spirit are groans only God can hear. The groans are the words you can't speak, all expressing themselves at once. When you can't find your way to the surface, when you can't open your mouth without inhaling more death, the deep of you cries to the deep of your Creator. No words are necessary between you.

Grief is a full-body experience. Your body, your mind, your heart, and your spirit are all processing the loss of something you loved that's no longer present. We tend to have a narrow definition of grief, reserving it for the death of a loved one. But grief is much more multifaceted than that. Even when we lose a person, we aren't just grieving the loss of their life but the loss of all that their life held and would have held. There are less obvious griefs too, like losing a job or moving away from family or from a place we felt connected to. We grieve when our kids hit a milestone and enter a new stage. We grieve the passing of time. Grief is as much a part of the human experience as breathing.

Grief is a full-body experience.

It's also one of our most powerful connections to our Creator. God's Word tells us that he's close to the brokenhearted and saves the crushed in spirit.* When God entered our world as a human, he experienced every human emotion. He grieved when his friend died, and he was so obviously upset that those around him noticed his spirit was troubled and "moved." Just before he cleansed the Temple, he grieved for the city of Jerusalem.† The Greek word for "wept" in this verse, *klaió*, implies that he was weeping audibly.[4]

In the garden of Gethsemane, just before his death, he grieved so intensely that not only was he sweating but those beads of sweat turned into blood.‡ Do you know how much anguish you have to be in for your body to push blood through the pores of your skin? The condition is called hematohidrosis, and it's brought on by extreme amounts of stress—think soldiers-in-battle kind of stress.[5]

The grief of Jesus was always a physical experience. The writers of the Gospels couldn't read his mind—they noticed his grief because they saw and heard his physical responses to it.

Isaiah prophesied that the Messiah would be a man of many sorrows, acquainted with grief.§ Yet we are so uncomfortable with our own grief that when it comes to prayer and spiritual formation, we try to bypass it. We think of grief as a hurdle to overcome instead of a sacred part of our walk with Christ. Jesus wept openly and unashamedly. He allowed his body to process grief the way it needed to. He was honest with his Father in his anguish, modeling how we can approach heaven with our deepest sorrows.

In the garden, when blood was dripping from the sweat glands of his body, Jesus asked God to change the plan: "My Father, if it is possible, may this cup be taken from me. Yet not as I will, but as you will."¶ The next day, when he was dying on the cross, he cried out, "My God, my God, why have you forsaken me?"** He was

---

* *Psalm 34:18*
† *Luke 19:41*
‡ *Luke 22:39-44*
§ *Isaiah 53:3*
¶ *Matthew 26:39*
** *Mark 15:34*

echoing the words of David, and in doing so, echoing the cries of every heart that's been broken.

The deep of Christ calling out to the deep of his Father.

✳

One of the core tenets of Christian belief is hope. When grief comes our way, it feels like a direct threat to that hope. So we throw a blanket over our pain and look to the future for a celestial utopia, where our tears will be wiped away forever.

Of course we do! We're eager for an existence that isn't accompanied by pain. We weren't created for pain, so naturally we want to escape it. But when we only set our eyes toward the end, we fail to see the movement of God in and through our pain.

Grief reveals to us how ill-equipped we are on our own to process and handle our pain. It makes our spirits and our bodies feel broken and weak. But it's in our weakness that the strength of Christ is made perfect. Our weaknesses aren't liabilities to the Kingdom of God—they're assets. When we view our pain as something to be stewarded instead of escaped, we give Christ space to show his power and strength—not in spite of what's happened to us, but through it.

We don't have to hide how deeply we've been affected by terrible things. That's because the Kingdom of God doesn't prioritize strength the way the world does. In God's Kingdom, true strength is displayed through Christ's power in our weakness, not in our ability to power through the things that make our souls weak.

> The distance between our grief and the throne room of heaven closes when we let our heartbreak breathe.

As much as we may want to stuff down our sadness and hide our weakness, we need to allow our spirits to groan and grieve and cry out. We need to give our bodies permission to hold on to and release the grief however they need to. The distance between our grief and the throne room of heaven closes when we let our heartbreak breathe. As we release our emotions, like Jesus did, we enter that same sacred space.

The veil between heaven and earth isn't as thick as we think. That's never more obvious than when the deep of us is crying out to the deep of God.

Sometimes prayer is nothing more than holding our grief in front of God. With slumped shoulders and trembling hands, we yearn for God to see our pain and offer a salve for it. The weight of grief makes our knees buckle, and we collapse under it. We can hear people shouting, "Get up! Stand strong! Petition the throne!" But God says simply, "Be still."

Prayer is a posture of the heart, a groan from the pit of our spirits. When we are still before the Lord, we can receive from him indiscriminately. When we set aside our expectations of what we think we're owed, we can open our hearts to accept what he has for us.

We can't hear him if we do all the talking, so sometimes we need to let our spirits do the praying. Getting quiet helps us attune to our own hearts as we attune to the Holy Spirit. The chaos of grief and suffering can fill our minds with spiritual and emotional clutter. But in the stillness, he can make our burdens light.

❋

Sometimes it seems like our prayers have been lost on the floor of heaven, ignored by the one who promised to come when we called.

C. S. Lewis described this heart-wrenching experience in the first few pages of *A Grief Observed*: "Go to Him when your need is desperate, when all other help is in vain, and what do you find?

A door slammed in your face, and a sound of bolting and double bolting on the inside. After that, silence. You may as well turn away.

Sometimes prayer is nothing more than holding our grief in front of God.

The longer you wait, the more emphatic the silence will become. There are no lights in the windows. It might be an empty house. Was it ever inhabited? It seemed so once."[6]

There are times in our grief when it feels like God is a million miles away. We pound on the door of heaven with our requests, and when we don't get what we asked for, we feel abandoned and forgotten. We hold up our image of who God should be and how he should respond to us, and we interpret his silence as a total lack of movement.

Suffering forces us to relearn what it means to pray—and why we pray at all. What's the point of presenting our requests before God if not to move him to change our circumstances? Why cry out at all if he won't respond? Prayer seems simple . . . until it doesn't.

We've all been given formulas for prayer: "You need to pray in faith, without wavering." "You need to partner prayer with fasting." "You need to pray while kneeling to show your submission." "You need to pray with certain words." But grief has a way of pulling the prayer rug right out from under our feet.

When pain steals your words and weakens your body, and you barely have the desire to breathe, much less pray, does God turn his face from you because you aren't saying the right words? Does he ignore the prayers of those whose bodies are bound to their beds because they can't kneel? Does he turn his face from us because we didn't check all the right boxes? Do we have to crack a secret code to bend God's ear?

When we put all these limitations on our prayers, we're ultimately making God as small as we are. He exists outside of formulas, and he isn't shackled by our systems. When we don't get the answer we were looking for, maybe it isn't that God's not present but that he's not present in the way we want him to be.

Prayer can be as simple as attuning to the presence of God and communicating with him in that sacred space between what can be seen and what cannot.

We forget that our requests are just that—requests—and that prayer is more than our asks. Prayer is the way we commune with the divine.

Hearts that are turned toward heaven don't always need to speak. They don't necessarily need to submit their requests. Prayer can be as simple as attuning to the presence of God and communicating with him in that sacred space between what can be seen and what cannot.

God doesn't need our words to know our hearts. He hears our spirits, and he knows our hearts. He is present with us in our groanings. When we can untangle ourselves from our expectations, we'll be able to truly know him, as he knows us.

Acts 17:27-29 says that God isn't far from each of us and that because we're his offspring, we're not like something made of gold or silver or stone, "an image fashioned by human art and imagination" (CSB). Our spirits are intangibly connected to his because it's in him that we live and move and have our being. His divine nature (and therefore the divine nature reflected in us) is beyond the boundaries of our human imagination.

In our attempts to understand God and move him, we try so hard to fashion him into our image and make him like us. We are uncomfortable in the mysteries of God, and prayer exists in that mystery. But God never asked us to make sense of his ways or pin him down or figure out the exact formula for faith. He just asks us to take a step, even when it doesn't make sense.

Instead of trying to define prayer, explain it, and do it "right," maybe instead we just need to pray. Remember that God is kind and merciful. He isn't standing at a distance watching us flail around as we try to pray the right way. He isn't some terrible manager watching us make mistakes and silently shaking his head, disappointed in us, but never showing us another way.

Our words are never abandoned at his feet, and he doesn't turn his back on us when we don't have words at all. He pulls us in, holds us tight, comforts us, and lightens the burdens that are breaking our backs.

THE DISTORTION:

Prayer is a transaction between the
created and the Creator: for forgiveness,
for healing, or for something tangible.

THE SHIFT:

Prayer is more than a transaction—more than
requests or words. It's a posture toward heaven
that allows us to connect with the divine.

7

The Risk of Engagement

Who can take away suffering without entering it?

HENRI NOUWEN

I EXPERIENCED MOST OF THE LAST HALF of my pregnancy alone. I went to appointments alone. I was alone during my multiple emergency room visits for high blood pressure and preterm labor.

The months in between the ultrasound and our delivery are a blur. At first I was being seen by my doctors once a week, then twice a week, then three times a week. Each week included an hour-long ultrasound. Some weeks the doctors would look at the blood flow and the babies' cords and say, "Wow! They're doing better than we expected!" only to tell me at the next scan that things were dire and we would need to act soon.

At twenty-six weeks along, I was diagnosed with gestational hypertension, a condition that's common with twin pregnancies. It can quickly lead to preeclampsia, which is extremely dangerous for the mother, resulting in seizures, strokes, and even death. At that point, we were closer to the viability age for the babies, and we had to dance the line between what was safest for the babies and what was safest for me. For the babies, of course, it was best to remain in utero as long as possible. But every week I stayed pregnant increased the risk of stroke and death for me. It was a delicate balance of risk to the babies and risk for me.

When I went into preterm labor, Zach wasn't allowed into the hospital until the doctors determined whether I would be admitted. He slept on the floor between two sets of automatic doors because he wanted to be as close as possible if I ended up being rushed to surgery.

I was admitted a few days later due to my hypertension, which was becoming increasingly severe, and because Baby B had started to experience reverse blood flow—the main fear for her.

At twenty-seven weeks, I was hospitalized indefinitely. The plan was to keep a close eye on the babies and me, with the hope that we'd make it to thirty-two weeks and have a planned C-section. But I went into labor (for real this time) two weeks later.

I was alone for almost all of it. Between COVID restrictions and the need to care for our three other children, Zach was rarely able to be with me. He came by once a day to bring food, drop off mail, and spend a few minutes with me, but other than that, I was alone on the high-risk floor of labor and delivery.

I decided to turn my hospital room into a cozy little suite. I pretended it was a New York City studio, and I think that helped me not go totally crazy in there. I requested a microwave and a fridge, and I was able to make most of my meals myself. This was a necessity, because the hospital food was, to put it mildly, atrocious.

It took less than twenty-four hours for the saltless, flavorless (and definitely defrosted) meals to send me into a spiral of depression and anger about my situation. I was separated from my kids, away from my husband, isolated in a hospital room, and carrying the emotional and mental weight of not knowing if I'd be leaving this hospital alone or with my babies. *And* I had to eat gray pork chops and powdered mashed potatoes? No sir.

People in crisis deserve to eat well. Casseroles, ideally. Dinner casseroles, dessert casseroles, breakfast casseroles—preferably from an old Southern woman who doesn't know what cholesterol is or why it matters. Chipotle burritos with the exact proportion of meat to rice. Arroz con pollo made by your Puerto Rican neighbor, who once yelled at you when she caught you using a rice maker. Biscuits dipped in thick sausage gravy that you intentionally get on your fingers just so you can them lick it off. Sweet tea that's brewed, not from a powdered mix (blech!). Chocolate cake with frosting that coats the inside of your stomach. Tikka masala from the Indian restaurant that you frequent so much they know you by name. Chicken kabobs from the Lebanese place where the owner comes out to shake your hand because you ordered sixty kabobs to eat throughout the week.

When people are nose to nose with tragedy, give them food that nourishes their bodies as well as their souls. Why should they have to decide what their next meal will be when they have to make much more taxing decisions? No one has the energy to make good diet decisions when they're in crisis. When you're just trying to survive from one day to the next, your body is the least of your concerns.

But I digress.

Every now and then, I'd have a FaceTime hangout with a friend, but for the most part, I was socially isolated. I looked forward to "visits" with my nurse friends. Unfortunately for them, they were my only social interaction outside of Zach and the occasional virtual chat with a friend.

I got used to seeing the same faces each day, and I had a routine with each person on my medical team. I am fully an introvert, which was helpful in isolation, but toward the end of my hospital quarantine, my social behavior got a little questionable. At one point at least, I was the topic of conversation around the nurse's desk, because I told a story about a can of vegetables that I thought was really funny, but I guess it wasn't funny at all. I told it to three different nurses, just to make sure. I was hoping one of them would think it was as funny as I did, but none of them really got the humor in it. I don't even remember what the story was, but we still have the can of vegetables.

After the last sympathy giggle from one of my nurses, I texted one of my nurse friends and said, "I think I'm starting to forget how to interact with people, and I'm pretty sure they're talking about me at the desk." She assured me that yes, they were without a doubt laughing at me. It's a humbling reminder that with enough isolation, even introverts can talk too much.

Anyway, I loved my nurses. And I think they loved me too. I know it's probably their job to make me feel that way, and I know that when they interact with patients, they aren't there to make friends. But I also know that nurses have favorite patients, and I like to think I made it to the top of a few of their lists, despite the weird vegetable can story.

There were two nurses in particular I grew attached to: Kim, my overnight nurse, and Katie, who had the day shift. I was comfortable with them and trusted them. They asked me about my family, they remembered what I liked and didn't like, and they'd bring up conversations from days before and remember the tiniest details. Three times a day, they'd strap the heart rate monitor to my belly, and we'd sit together, sometimes for hours, while they chased heartbeats.

So of course, the day I went into labor was the day neither of them was working. I had two new nurses who were fantastic, but they weren't *my* nurses. They didn't know me. They didn't know my babies the way Kim and Katie did. They didn't get my sarcasm or my fears. They hadn't reassured me or checked in on me or asked how my kids were doing over the past three weeks. They hadn't even heard the can of vegetables story! We'd just met, and now they were going to help bring my babies into the world.

✳

It was the evening of Mother's Day, and the hospital had just changed their COVID visitor policy, so my mother-in-law was able to stop in for a quick visit. While we were talking, I had a sudden, intense headache that grew more and more painful over the next few hours.

I paged my nurse, and he strapped me to the fetal monitors and ordered blood work to look for signs of preeclampsia.

Not long after my headache hit, I started contracting. I was seeing stars, my head was throbbing, and my back felt like someone was prodding it with a metal rod. All things that pointed to being in active labor.

A few minutes after strapping the monitors to my belly, the nurse came back in a rush. "Are you feeling those?"

"YES!" I'd been in labor so many times that I knew what this was, and I knew it would go fast. My labors always did.

Less than forty-five minutes after paging my nurse, I'd progressed to three centimeters and had begun leaking amniotic fluid. My cervix was opening at a rapid rate.

Zach was thirty-five minutes away, putting our kids in bed, when the doctor sat down on my bed.

"We're having these babies right now," she said.

I burst into tears. I was so scared. It was too early. I really wanted to make it to thirty-two weeks. Zach wasn't here. I'd never had surgery before. I wasn't ready. *They* weren't ready.

The room filled with faces I'd never seen before, and they pumped me full of drugs to offset the effects of preeclampsia and to prepare my body for a C-section.

The doctor assured me that the babies looked great. "I wish *all* the babies on the floor tonight were doing as well as yours are right now," she told me. A slight consolation. It was still too early. I was just twenty-nine weeks that day.

I texted Zach, "You need to get here. I'm 3 cm."

"Wait, what?"

"They're calling my doctor to come. The babies are doing well. But they're coming tonight."

"Okay. I'm waking up the kids."

"They're gonna start prepping me. Babe, you need to hurry."

"I'm coming. Sixteen minutes away."

"Okay. IV is in. Magnesium drip."

"Ten minutes away."

Zach made it to the hospital as they were unlatching the wheels of my bed to take me to the OR.

They told me it would feel like pressure, but I felt everything. I was wailing in pain, so the anesthesiologist kept upping the dose. I was slipping in and out of consciousness, aware of what was happening, but only just.

Chloe came out first and cried immediately. Lydia was quiet.

I heard my doctor say, "Come on, Lydia. Come on baby. Let us hear you cry."

It felt like an eternity, but she finally let out the sweetest little cry. She sounded like a kitten. The room erupted in cheers.

I heard a nurse giggle. "They just had to be born on different days, didn't they?"

Chloe was born at 11:59 p.m., and Lydia was born at 12:01 a.m. Twins born two minutes apart, on separate days. Because of course they would.

I caught a glimpse of their plastic beds as the NICU nurses wheeled them away. The nurses were calm, but they moved quickly. I felt numb. I knew my babies were in the beds, but my mind and my body hadn't connected the fact that they had been born. In a way, it felt like watching someone else's babies being wheeled away.

After surgery, I was brought back to the room I'd been in for three weeks, only to be whisked off to another floor the next day. I was far from my nurse friends and the comfort of my little hospital studio apartment.

I hadn't been able to hold my babies yet. I was still recovering from the twenty-four-hour magnesium drip, a treatment for preeclampsia that prevents seizures and strokes. I unaffectionately refer to it as Satan's spit, and I hope you never have the misfortune of having your body being infected with its lifesaving poison. You know how you feel when you get a stomach bug but you haven't started throwing up yet? It feels like that. Unrelenting nausea and brain fog. Misery in an IV bag.

My body was reeling from the aftereffects of major surgery, nausea from the magnesium, withdrawal from medications that were making me throw up all over myself, and wild hormonal changes. Worst of all, I was separated from my babies, who were strapped to breathing tubes and feeding tubes, and who were so tiny I thought they might break if I touched them.

I sat on my new bed in my new room and tried to get settled. The new nurses came in and immediately strapped the blood pressure device onto my arm. For three weeks, I'd been having blood pressure checks every two hours, twenty-four hours a day, and one of my arms had some nerve damage and bruising as a result. That's the arm they strapped the cuff to.

I shouted in pain and ripped off the cuff. "No. I'm done," I said. "No more checks. Please get out of my room."

The pressure that had been building up in me was nearing the surface. I was an Instant Pot, and my lid was about to blow off.

The nurses scolded me, because a preeclampsia patient can't just opt out of blood pressure checks. I let them put the cuff on the other arm, and unsurprisingly, my blood pressure was through the roof.

The nurses started telling me about all the procedures and checks they were going to do—things I'd just been told I wouldn't have to do anymore. *I can't do this for another week,* I thought.

I was holding it together, waiting for them to leave the room. But then they told me I'd probably get a roommate. That's when my brain broke. Everything broke.

I'd held myself together for three months, trying to get from one day to the next. I'd internalized every fear and panicked thought and tried to protect everyone around me from feeling the weight of what I was carrying. Every ounce of that emotional restraint came bursting out in that hospital room that felt like an asylum. I was broken. Well, I'd already been broken. It was just on the outside now.

I was crying the way kids do when they don't have emotional regulation and can't tell you what's really wrong. The groaning, screeching, trying to talk but not forming any discernible words kind of cry. My crying turned to hyperventilating, and I yelled at everyone to get out of my room and leave me alone.

It was completely out of character for me, but these nurses didn't know that. They didn't know me. They gave each other knowing looks and refused to leave. They ignored me and kept poking and prodding, getting their readings, checking their lists, and calling me the wrong name.

After becoming so familiar with the other team, I was now a nobody when I really, really needed to be somebody to *someone.*

Zach had been taking some of my things to the car, so he wasn't there for my breakdown. He just saw the aftermath. He walked into the room where he'd left a calm wife and came back to someone who was absolutely losing her mind.

He tried to piece together what had happened, but I was too upset to explain. All at once, his face changed. He'd been bottling things up too.

My husband is the most soft-spoken, patient person I've ever known. No one has ever had a negative thing to say about my husband. But a hysterical wife in an already fragile state in a place where she should feel safe and cared for was too much for him.

He practically ran to the nurses' station and gave them a piece of his mind. I couldn't hear what he was saying, but I heard him yell. I've never heard that man yell—before or since.

They were *definitely* talking about me at the nurse's station now.

Stepping into someone else's crisis is high risk and high reward. The emotional investment will always cost you something. But the reward is worth it. When you invest in someone's pain, it builds a trust that has little to do with personality or compatibility—it's the bond of sharing a painful experience with another person.

> Stepping into someone else's crisis is high risk and high reward.

We form emotional attachments to the people whose pain we carry and to those who carry ours. If you invest your time, your emotions, and your trust into each other, you feel connected for the rest of your lives. You become family.

One night after the girls were born, Zach and I were sitting in my hospital room eating dinner. The babies were in the NICU down the hall, and I was recovering from surgery. As we ate, I was telling Zach how much I missed my favorite nurses from the other floor. "I just wish I could see them again," I said.

The words had barely left my mouth when there was a knock at the door. I rolled my eyes and sent Zach to tell the nurse to come back later. But before he could get off his chair, Kim, my night nurse from the other floor, walked in.

She threw her arms in the air and made a joke about my not waiting until she came back from her long weekend to have the babies. I took one look at her face and burst into tears.

She ran over to me and ripped off her face mask. Then she sat on the edge of my bed, pulled me to her, and gave me the hug I'd been needing.

I sobbed into her shoulder. "They're so little."

She rubbed my back as she held me. "It's okay," she whispered. "It's okay that they're little."

Zach sat on the couch across from us, trying to become invisible to give us as much privacy as that small room allowed. He later told me he knew he was watching something sacred.

Zach held his breath and shed his own tears, for his own reasons. But this part of the experience was uniquely mine. I was the one who was hospitalized. I was the one getting poked and prodded twenty times a day. I was the one who had monitors strapped to my stomach as I wondered if they would show beating hearts or still ones. I was the one who had been left alone in a hospital room, separated from my kids, my husband, and the entire outside world, except for the few times a day when the nurses came in to take care of me.

But what a gift it was, for that moment, to share all the emotions with a nurse I barely knew but who understood what I was carrying. The bond between us was short, but it was sacred.

The story of Job is often used as an example of how *not* to be a friend to someone who's in crisis. We give Job's buddies such a hard time, and honestly I get it. They were rude, arrogant, victim blaming, and completely wrong in their assessment of why God had allowed Job to experience so much tragedy.

I used to read that story and think about what jerks they were. But after I went through some pretty difficult things, I found myself wishing I had friends like Job.

Let me explain.

Job was a man with an abundance of wealth, family, and reasons for joy. Scripture describes him as a man of God and a man of perfect integrity. Then Satan came to God and was like, "Yeah, of course he's a man of God—look at how easy you've made his life. Take all that away, and he'll curse you."

And God says, "Challenge accepted." (Paraphrase, of course, but you get it.) God allowed Satan to take everything from Job. His cattle, his children, his workers—everything. He went from being a man who had everything to a man with absolutely nothing.

But that wasn't enough. Job was then infected with boils from the top of his head to the soles of his feet. He was so miserable that he used broken pottery to scratch his skin. Even his wife was like, "Put yourself out of your misery and curse God so he'll kill you."

Job refused.

That's where his three friends came in.

Eliphaz, Bildad, and Zophar heard what had happened to their friend, and they came to sympathize with him and comfort him. The text says that they wept, tore their robes, threw dust in the air, and sat with Job for seven days and seven nights. They didn't speak a word because "they saw that his suffering was very intense."* For

---

* *Job 2:13*, CSB

seven days and seven nights, they sat in silence with their grieving, tormented friend. In their silence, they honored his tragedy.

Maybe that's why, when they finally spoke, Job allowed them to say so much. The trust they'd earned by sharing his grief earned them the right to speak what they believed to be true about his circumstances.

We tend to skip over the significance of offering brotherly love to someone who is suffering—both in Job's story and in living our lives with each other. Job's friends were good friends to him in their display of solidarity and shared grief. But then they started talking. Eliphaz let Job know that he believed that God only punishes the wicked, so surely this tragedy happened because Job had done something wrong.

He landed a particularly low blow when he said, "His children are far from safety, they are crushed in the gate, there is no one to save them." He completely dismissed Job's lifetime of being a loving father, not only to his own children but to orphans as well. He cared deeply for his children, even going so far as to offer sacrifices for them, just in case they needed a little extra forgiveness. To tell a loving father that his now dead children were never safe with him is cruel. But let's give Eliphaz the benefit of the doubt. Maybe he was just trying to "speak the truth in love."

The next friend, Bildad, said basically the same thing but blamed Job's children for their own deaths. He essentially said that they were dead because of their sin. He told Job that all he needed to do was repent of whatever he'd done wrong, and God would restore everything he'd lost. He used logic and what he believed to be true about God based on what he'd seen and experienced. He couldn't fathom that someone righteous would suffer the way Job suffered, so he reasoned that there was something Job needed to repent of.

Then we have Zophar, the most hotheaded friend of the

three. He was snarky, and his words were sharp and mean. He agreed with the other two, saying that God was punishing Job for his wickedness. He was angry that Job insisted on his innocence, and he used fear and threats to try to break Job's confidence that he hadn't done anything wrong. His words were harsh and merciless.

Eventually, all three friends gave up on saying anything to Job because "he is righteous in his own eyes." That's when Elihu (not sure where he came from or why he was there) steps in. Elihu waited until everyone was done talking, likely because he fancied himself the wisest of the bunch. He was like a recent Bible school grad: full of knowledge, but not a lick of wisdom to be found. He went on and on, saying things like, "Be patient with me a little longer, and I will inform you, for there is still more to be said on God's behalf. I will get my knowledge from a distant place and ascribe justice to my Maker. Indeed, my words are not false; one who has complete knowledge is with you."*

Ugh. Are we all rolling our eyes right now? Elihu annoys me more than anyone else in this story because he's so arrogant, but he thinks he's humble. Elihu didn't rebuke Job's sinful behavior as the cause of his family's demise and the loss of his wealth; he rebuked Job for the way he was responding to it. He told Job how he *should* respond to suffering and rebuked him for not graciously, humbly accepting this as discipline from God. What an astonishing display of arrogance.

This story concludes with God rebuking Job's friends for misrepresenting him. They were wrong. They repented and God forgave them, as God does.

This is an ancient story, but it's all too relatable for anyone who has walked through something hard. If you're lucky enough

---

* *Job 36:1-4*, CSB

to have a community that cares for you, you'll bump into people with every good intention who offer incredibly misguided advice.

When something tragic happens, we try to make sense of it any way we can. We want to find a reason for it so we can escape it. We try to find an explanation for suffering in the life of someone who is good because it's too difficult to accept that sometimes people just suffer. There has to be a reason.

In Job's story, the people who spoke into his situation were wrong. *So* wrong. They misrepresented the character of God and spoke falsely against Job. The best thing they did was bear witness to his pain in silence for seven days.

But maybe the conversations between Job and his friends weren't all bad. When we have difficult confrontations with people who believe they are the mouthpiece of God in our pain, their words have a way of drawing truth from our hearts.

When someone accuses us of something, our natural response is to defend ourselves. When we make our case against the accusation, we evaluate and analyze our inner life against what our accuser is saying. As hurtful and unpleasant as it is to be accused and blamed, the process of defending ourselves helps us develop a sense of clarity about who we are and what is true.

We can take words that are harmful and use them as a catalyst to search ourselves and better understand the mysteries of God.

God's Word never instructs us to rush past our pain. We're never told to disregard it. We're never told to ignore it. God doesn't consider pain weak or inappropriate.

When we see someone who is hurting, they don't need criticism. They don't need a sermon. What they need is someone to just be with them. Hope can be held by broken hearts, and it can also be given to hurting hearts by whole ones. We give hope to others when we truly see each other, when we bear witness to each other's pain.

As we do so, we remind each other of our divine image. When I am bearing witness, I see the image of God reflected in the way they hold their pain, express it, honor it, and trust the Lord with it. When I am the one hurting, I see God's kindness and comfort reflected in the way someone listens to and cares for me.

❋

Shortly after I had my third baby, we moved to my husband's home state of Massachusetts, where he was to serve as the youth pastor at his home church. We'd been a ministry team since we were nineteen years old. We'd been youth pastors, worship leaders, jack-of-all-trades pastors—always together. Always a team. This was the first time in our married lives that we weren't seen as a duo. He was on staff, and I was his wife. He went to work, and I stayed home.

With that move, every dynamic in our relationship and our home life shifted. We were like two pieces of paper that had been glued together, set out to dry, and then unceremoniously ripped apart. We didn't know how to function as a team when we weren't doing the same work, side by side, day in and day out.

I felt like he was moving forward without me. I was jealous that he got to be a pastor and have a career and be his own person while I stayed home and raised his kids. I felt betrayed, even though it was an agreed-upon betrayal.

I fell into a quick—and deep—depression. I was overwhelmed by having three children four years old and under, with very little help at home. We only had one car that he took to work every day, so I couldn't go out and join mom groups and make friends. I was the only stay-at-home mom at our church, and I felt out of place and silly among the women in our church who had careers. When I'd walk into church with my kids by my side, people would smile at them and say, "Hey, Mama!" I know they didn't mean it this way, but my loss of identity made me feel like they were mocking me. I stopped wearing my baby in a baby carrier because I thought if I didn't look "maternal," maybe people would call me by my name.

Sometimes I was so overwhelmed by the prospect of the day stretching out before me that I would cry in the broom closet in the morning, begging Zach not to go to work. He didn't know what to do with me. He just hoped I would get past whatever this was.

I didn't open up to many people about how I was feeling, mostly because I didn't understand it myself. I didn't know I was depressed. I didn't have the language to talk about what I was feeling and experiencing. The people who could tell something was off would offer little encouragements, like "When you move into your new house, it will be better!" Or "It's hard when the kids are little—it gets easier!" And perhaps the most crushing words: "We don't need you to help with anything at church. Just take care of those kids and yourself, and when you're feeling more settled, we'll find a place for you."

What was meant as empathy for my season of life made me feel unvalued and invisible. I hadn't yet accepted that my life had changed. Ministry was important to me, and I'd never considered how much having children would change the way that looked. I'd always had a job and a ministry and a purpose in our community. But this church didn't see that side of me. In some ways, it felt like they didn't see me at all. They saw Zach, and then they saw me as Zach's wife.

I felt like I had no value outside what I was able to do in my home. And because of my depression and anxiety, I didn't think that was very much. I was lonely and isolated, and the few encouraging words that came my way sent a clear message: "When you're better, we'll have a place for you—in the church, in relationships, in our lives. Until then, you're on your own, kid."

Years have passed and times have changed. I've been broken and healed and broken and healed a few more times. And although I've learned to function and developed healthier habits and coping skills, I'm still not completely past the struggles that surfaced so viscerally during that time. As far as thorns in the flesh go, anxiety and depression can be pretty chronic.

We're living in a time when just about everyone has experienced some kind of trauma, whether individual or collective. The thing about trauma is that it isn't something you just get past. It entirely rewires your brain, which means that most of us are walking around with brains that aren't in their original working order. We are chronically changed by the hardships we experience.

For some people, this surfaces in mental health issues that make it difficult to function and maintain relationships, jobs, or church responsibilities. But I wonder how different all our stories would be if we all had people who were just happy to be with us, no matter what.

Being transparent with another person about your own brokenness is one of the most terrifying of all human experiences. You don't feel brave or honest in vulnerability; you feel exposed. Most of us prefer to hide the darkness inside, because bringing it into the light puts us at risk of being judged and rejected. We are really good at hiding what we fear other people won't accept.

For the most part, people judge either because they don't understand or because they see themselves in your brokenness and aren't willing to face brokenness of their own. When we aren't willing to see our brokenness, we reject the brokenness in others.

After we left our church, I struggled with my faith in ways I never had before. God wasn't who I had believed him to be. The systems of my faith had failed me. I had been good, I had followed the rules, and I believed I'd been promised a victory. Yet we lost the battle. We'd been ostracized, rejected, isolated, and abandoned.

I felt like God had walked out on me and taken the side of my accusers. The bricks I'd built my faith on crumbled quickly. In the throes of that, I felt like I'd become a liability to everyone in my life. It wasn't like I *wanted* to have everything I believed explode in my face. I was crawling on the ground, gathering shards of beliefs, and trying to make sense of what had caused everything to blow up.

I *wanted* God to be who I'd thought he was. I wanted my theology to make sense. I wanted everything to be the same as it had always been. But it wasn't. My theology had been woven so tightly into the system of the church I'd been raised in that when I began to question the structures of the system, the threads of my theology began to loosen.

I looked at the structures of church authority I'd been raised to believe were biblical and compared them to the models of church described in the Bible. When I found those two weren't aligned the way I'd been taught, I began to pull at more and more threads.

I started asking uncomfortable questions, and I wasn't satisfied with simplistic answers. I was angry at God, angry at his people, and angry at myself. I wanted truth. I wanted to know God, truly and desperately. I was eager to discover who he really was, even if he wasn't who I thought he was.

Well-meaning friends and family warned me about the dangers of asking too many questions.

"Be careful," they would say in response to my questions. "That's a slippery slope."

They couldn't see that I was begging them to take me off the slope. *Give me some grippy socks or something, my goodness!*

Instead, some of my friends stepped away from a relationship with me. They stopped responding to my questions. They stopped following me on social media. The risk of being associated with someone like me—someone they thought might lose their orthodoxy—was too great.

One friend later told me, "I just needed to see where you were going with it. It wasn't clear at the time."

Well, it wasn't clear to me either! I was scrambling to get my faith to make sense again, and at the same time, I was losing my support system. My questions were too audacious. My emotions were too front and center. I was too messy with my pain, and people who loved me stopped engaging with it. I was a sheep without an earthly shepherd. Taking off to find the one lost sheep leaves the others exposed. And who will protect the flock from the wolves when that wayward sheep puts everyone at risk? What shepherd wants to deal with a sheep that's a flight risk when there are ninety-nine others that will fall in line?

I know of one.

Without anyone else willing to talk with me, the only voice I had was the voice of Jesus, the better Shepherd. He's pretty clear about the fact that he leaves the ninety-nine to save the one, but maybe it's unfair to expect anyone else to do the same.

We call the wandering sheep the "black sheep" of the flock. She's a bad influence, a troublemaker. But what if she didn't wander off on purpose? What if sheep from a rival flock came and tricked her? What if they beat her up until she could barely walk, much less find her way back to the shepherd? And what if the ninety-nine other sheep realized she was missing and said, "Hey, shepherd, let us go with you. She's our sister, and we can help you find her."

Thankfully for me, I ended up finding that flock of sheep that welcomed my questions, engaged with my doubts, and didn't rush me to any theological conclusions. They showed up in places you wouldn't expect to find a new flock. I found them by striking conversations with strangers in coffee shops and learning that we had a shared pain. I found them by following little nudges from the Holy Spirit to connect deeper with people I'd had only surface-level connections with before.

Slowly our "church" built around us, outside of the walls of a traditional church, with no formal gathering and no organized structure, just a handful of lost sheep being herded together by a Shepherd who knew we'd make a good flock.

There is so much healing that comes from being accepted as you are and not having to defend your pain. These friends saw my value to the Kingdom of God, even when I wasn't even sure what that meant anymore. They didn't wait for me to "get it together" before they'd engage with me. They walked with me, prayed with me, encouraged me, and gently supported the Shepherd's pursuit of me.

There is so much healing that comes from being accepted as you are and not having to defend your pain.

Even as I'm grateful for the healing that happened for me in the context of community, I recognize that doesn't happen for everyone. Many times we wander with our questions, feeling abandoned by our faith communities because they've determined that the risk of being associated with lost sheep is too high.

It's high risk to engage with and love a person who is wavering in their faith. And not just love in the "I'll always love you . . . from a distance" way, but in an up-close, in-your-face, willing-to-get-dirty way. Love in the way Jesus engaged with sinners and religious leaders, genuine followers and seekers. He broke all kinds of rules to further his Kingdom. He did so because he was so sure of who he was and what he was called to do that he didn't concern himself with what would happen if he had public relationships and interactions with people who were "risky."

⁂

I had vomit in my hair the first time I met Chloe and Lydia.

It was six hours after surgery. Every hour, I had begged to be taken to see them, but there weren't enough nurses available to roll my bed into the NICU. I had to be recovered enough to sit up and climb into a wheelchair. I tried to convince my medical team (and myself) that I was ready, even when I was still barely conscious. Between the magnesium drip, the pain medication, and the anesthesia, I could barely string words together other than "Can you take me now?"

When my nurse finally let me attempt to climb out of bed, I threw up all over my clothes, my bed, and my hair.

"Are you sure you're ready?" she asked me.

"Yeah, yeah, I'm fine, I'm fine." (I was not fine.)

She helped me stand and walked with me to my wheelchair, only for me to stop midway and throw up all over the floor, my legs, her shoes, and (once again) my hair.

"Maybe you should lay back down, and we'll try again in an hour."

"No way. Take me now."

There's a picture of me standing—just barely—at the foot of Chloe's NICU bed. You can see the nurses, both mine and the babies', standing around me. You can see my finger cautiously stretched out to touch the bottom of Chloe's foot, because I wasn't sure how else to touch her. You can see where the vomit soaked my hair and landed on my shoulder. You can see how miserable I felt and how, for the first time, the fear was taking over my body.

What you can't see is the nurse who looked at me from across the room and saw what no one else was paying attention to. She saw that my face was going white and that my hands were shaking, not because of the medication but because of the shock of seeing my babies for the first time.

They were so tiny, barely over two pounds each, and their faces were covered with wires and tubes. I couldn't see their eyes or the shape of their heads. Even their little noses were scrunched from the oxygen tubes in them. They looked cold and fragile. I was afraid to touch them, afraid to breathe too heavily. My knees started trembling. I must have stopped breathing altogether.

The nurse calmly walked over to me and stood next to me, shoulder to shoulder. For a few seconds, she didn't say anything. I know she could smell the sweat and vomit all over me. Those smells stand out in a sterile NICU.

She watched my face as I took it all in and very casually said, "They're in really good hands here. We're going to take good care of them."

She saw a broken, sick, hurting, *dirty* person walk into the room, and she responded to my pain by stepping closer to it. She endured my literal filth and stench and offered love and compassion—not because she had to but because she was compelled to. Her calm assurance gave me something to hold on to when I felt like the room and everything else was spinning out of control. She steadied me, with no consideration for her own comfort at all.

When we step away from people who are wrestling with aspects of their faith, is it because we don't trust God with our reputation?

Is he sovereign or not? Is he big enough and gracious enough to protect us when we love this brother or sister? Do we value our platforms and our image more than we value the soul of a sheep who has lost their way? What is the greater loss: what might happen if we ask too many questions or what might happen to a friend whose pain has shaken their faith into fragments over a scorched earth?

We can put the responsibility of faith and healing entirely on the person who is hurting. We can fill them with knowledge and "pour into them." We can teach from a distance; we can call them higher. We can detach ourselves from relationship with them and simply deliver the truth via a shared Instagram post or a sermon clip. But people aren't cups to be filled; they are plants to be cared for. People who are hurting need safe, nurturing environments where they can heal and grow. They need to be cared for specifically and on purpose.

There is risk in love, but this is what we're called to. The love Christ says we'll be known by is the kind of love that doesn't make sense to anyone outside the Kingdom of God. Even within it, sometimes. Christlike love is relentless and persistent. It's gentle and strong, kind and good.

> There is risk in love, but this is what we're called to.

We are called to love each other without reservation or restriction, as Christ loves us. God's Word doesn't give us a step-by-step flowchart of the right behaviors and actions to take when someone is hurting. But Christ modeled what love for our brothers and sisters in Christ should look like.

It looks like inconvenience.

It looks like sacrifice.

It may even look like following the Shepherd to find where the lost sheep wandered off to.

THE DISTORTION:
I need to keep those who are struggling with their faith at a distance.

❋

THE SHIFT:
Engaging with someone's pain and doubts might cost me something, but I am called and equipped to love them, nurture them, and lead them to the safety of the Good Shepherd.

When Joy Locks Hands with Grief

Our life is . . . a time in which sadness and
joy kiss each other at every moment.

HENRI NOUWEN

IF I'D HAD A TIME MACHINE when I was fifteen years old and been given a glimpse of my life twenty years in the future, I would have been overjoyed at how many chances I'd have to "suffer for Jesus." Younger me would have looked at the future trauma and eaten it right up. A crisis pregnancy? Premature babies? "Choosing life" in the face of death? I would have jumped at the chance to prove my faith in the face of terrible circumstances. I fancied myself quite the little martyr and would have slept well each night knowing that one day I'd get a chance to bleed out for Jesus.

I was a teenager at the height of an era in Christian youth culture that glorified martyrdom. The 1990s and early 2000s were a strange time to be a young Christian. We all wanted to be like the martyrs of Columbine. The band DC Talk released a book about martyrs and had us all calling ourselves "Jesus freaks." The Left

Behind series shaped our theology more than God's Word did, and we lived in constant fear of missing the Rapture. To us, the ultimate act of declaring our love for Jesus (and securing a ticket into heaven) was to die a brave death while refusing to deny our Lord and Savior.

When I tell you I fantasized about this, I'm not exaggerating in the slightest. As often as I would stand in front of my full-length mirror holding a hairbrush and pretending to sing to a crowd of adoring fans, I would stand in front of that same mirror, on my knees, rehearsing my last words at my execution speech. It didn't feel like pretend; it felt inevitable. I was *excited* about it. I wouldn't deny Jesus, even in my last breath!

My journals are filled with the hope that my adolescent writings would be published and reach the world for Christ after my death. I would be like Anne Frank, unknown while I was alive but famous in my death.

My death would serve as a catalyst to revival. Thousands would come to my funeral, and all of them would respond to the altar call I would make sure my dad gave before they lowered me into the ground. I was ready.

"Take my life, Lord," I wrote. "I am consecrated to thee"—as if I knew what any of that meant.

Take teenage angst and mix it with a bit of theological convolution, and you get a generation of earnest Christian kids begging for trauma and death to prove their love for Christ.

On top of my desire to die for Jesus, I had Christian mentors who told me that my knack for getting in trouble, disobeying, and getting caught in lies revealed a battle for my soul. They'd say things like "God must have big plans for you, Kristen, or the devil wouldn't be trying so hard to stop them."

So I believed not only that the devil was on my back, but that he was there because God had big plans for me—plans so big they would disrupt some kind of evil enemy plot. That's a lot of spiritual weight for a kid to shoulder.

Whenever something bad happened, I assumed the devil was trying to stop God's plan. Suffering was proof that I was important to God. If I didn't matter to God, he would ignore me and my life would be peaceful, quiet, and boring. As a kid, I found the idea of a boring life horrifying. As an adult, after experiencing enough trauma, I'm kind of envious of a life like that. Boring starts to sound really great after a couple of traumas.

The first time I was confronted with the fault in this theology was the summer before my junior year of college. I was doing an internship in Paraguay with my uncle, who was the national youth director for our denomination at the time. I lived in a tiny apartment with another girl from the US. Our apartment was so tiny that we shared a full-size bed. I've been married for fifteen years, and if we stay somewhere where we have to share anything less than a queen, we're not sharing a bed. It's simply not happening. So this was already spiritual warfare for me.

During one of our ministry outings, we served at an outdoor program where we gave out food, organized games, and offered crafts and story time to kids in the neighborhood. There were probably a hundred and fifty kids to our thirty or so adults, and we spent most of the day with kids on our backs and in our laps. They played with our hair, did our makeup, and showered us with hugs. It was a full-contact kind of day. There was no thought of germs—we were just loving on kids for Jesus.

A few days later, my co-intern, the one I shared a tiny bed with, found lice in her hair.

Neither one of us had seen lice before, and we were as dramatic as two nineteen-year-old girls can be—screaming, gagging, and freaking out. I spent hours with a lice comb, pulling bugs out of my roommate's hair and washing them down the drain.

I prepared myself for the inevitability that I'd be combing lice out of my hair soon too. But as luck would have it, I never got a single egg or bug in my hair. Not one. I don't know if it was because I'd just dyed my hair or if it was some benevolent mercy, but somehow those bugs didn't jump from her head to mine, even while I slept next to her with our heads practically touching.

Not. One. Bug.

Later that month, we shared our harrowing story with some youth pastors from the US, and one of them made a comment about how the lice proved that my friend was truly a servant of the Lord. The enemy was attacking her, and she was suffering for Jesus.

I agreed, nodding my head at the sentiment, and thought about the sacrifice my friend had made. She'd come to this country, given so much of herself to these children, and then suffered the consequences. Then I thought, *Wait a minute. Why didn't I get lice? Am I not suffering for Jesus?*

We were doing the same things together every day. We went to the same places, ate the same food, and had the same jobs. Everything was the same—everything. (Let's not fail to acknowledge that I was the one who was helping comb lice out of her hair, which I think is a notable level of suffering too. But I digress.)

I came to the conclusion that there must be something lacking in my heart. She must have been doing something that I wasn't doing. Some posture, some sacrifice, *something*. Otherwise, I would have lice too. Instead of being relieved that I didn't have lice, I was ashamed. I felt like it exposed me as a fraud.

Imagine being in a foreign country and *wishing* you had lice! In another world, under other circumstances, somebody would have said God's favor spared me, but not in my case.

So I prayed fervently, *"Let me suffer for you, Jesus. Give me lice!"*

What twisted tales we tell ourselves when we try to make our theology feed our egos. I didn't want to suffer for Jesus to bring glory to him—I wanted to suffer for him so I could be as good of a Christian as my friend who had been given the blessing of lice. I wanted to know that God approved of me, and I thought that having hundreds of bugs crawling through my hair would be proof of that. Even after I combed the darn things out of her hair while saying, "Oh my gosh, ew" for hours, that's what I wanted for my life. *I wanted bugs.*

We get so insecure about our relationship with God sometimes. We want tangible proof that we're doing okay. Through a series of theological misunderstandings and exaggerations, we've mistakenly believed that people who suffer most are the most important in the Kingdom of God. I once heard a pastor say, "Your suffering in life is directly proportional to your significance in the Kingdom of God." I'm sorry, *what*? To be significant, we have to suffer? I mean, first of all, why are we seeking significance? Jesus was pretty clear about the last being first and the least becoming the greatest.[*] Second, who says God can only use us if we're suffering? Yes, God uses us in our suffering, but this is not a litmus test for his favor.[†]

This idea that God chooses his bravest soldiers for his biggest battles is nonsense! What kind of father would take his most cherished or "significant" children and torture them? We seem to have forgotten that we have a heavenly Father who delights in giving good gifts to his children.[‡]

It's a sign that we've strayed a long way from the heart of the Father when we start expecting pain and are caught off guard by his goodness. We grow suspicious of joy and wait for the other shoe to fall, revealing the pain we know isn't far behind. We view

---

[*] *Matthew 20:16; 19:13-15*
[†] *Philippians 4:12*
[‡] *Luke 11:13*

joy as a temporal state while waiting for the next round of suffering to come our way.

Ugh. Can you imagine how much it must grieve the Father to have us yearning for pain when he has promised us joy and abundance?

⁂

The first chapter of James says, "Consider it great joy, my brothers and sisters, whenever you experience various trials." Christians often quote this to comfort themselves or to correct someone's emotional response to what they're going through. "This is difficult, but consider it joy!" It's one of those flippant, dismissive things people say without really knowing what the verse means.

It's sad that something that should be good can be manipulated into something that heaps guilt and shame onto someone who's hurting. It's good to remind each other of who we are and what we have in Christ, but we need to be careful about the way we communicate and deliver these messages. Sometimes a well-meaning point toward joy can come across as dismissive to someone who needs more than a pithy phrase.

Before we tell someone to think of the crushing pain in their life as joy, we should be able to describe what joy actually is. The kind of joy we can have when we're suffering isn't a joy that bypasses our emotions. Joy doesn't have to ignore emotion, because it *isn't* an emotion.

Heartbreak can cast a dark shadow over every good thing, but true joy is an inward gladness that doesn't depend on circumstances. It isn't so much something we feel as something we're postured toward. It's a unilateral gladness that's given to everyone who belongs to God: rich and poor, sick and healthy, male and female, young and old. Joy is part of the very character of God, and it's mercifully extended to us who are made in his image.

Joy is a gift God gives us as we trust him with our life,[*] and it can't be taken away. No feeling we experience is strong enough to put an obstacle in front of the joy we have as children of God. *That* joy isn't going anywhere.

It's crucial to separate true joy from emotions so we don't use the call to be joyful as an excuse to ignore what we're actually feeling or to elevate our suffering as something to be happy about. When James said to "consider it joy," he wasn't saying that we should get excited about suffering.

Imagine walking up to the disciples and saying, "Good news! You're going to be beheaded! You're going to be crucified upside down! You're going to be stoned to death! Isn't that great?" What kind of faith looks at suffering and says, "Yes! Finally!" A masochistic one, that's what kind.

And yet we have to wrestle with some strange passages about suffering in Scripture. Jesus said that people who mourn are blessed.[†] Peter said we should rejoice in sharing Christ's sufferings.[‡] Paul rejoiced in his sufferings and boasted in his weaknesses.[§] This is the same guy who called his trials (which included beatings and arrests) "light momentary affliction."[¶] I know my experiences might pale in comparison to others', but I'd never call them "light" or "momentary."

We've taken these words in Scripture, which were intended to frame the meaning of suffering in a believer's life, and misconstrued them to elevate hardships and idolize those who suffer. Theology like this keeps people stuck in catastrophe. Why would

---

[*] *Romans 15:13*
[†] *Matthew 5:4*
[‡] *1 Peter 4:12-13*
[§] *Colossians 1:24*
[¶] *2 Corinthians 4:17,* ESV

we ever want peace, healing, or rest if suffering is proof of God's attention and approval? When we believe that suffering is a sign of God's approval, we can't be at peace unless we're in pain.

※

When our girls were in the NICU, there was a particular sentiment people expressed that made me feel the lowest of lows. They'd say, "I don't know how you do it. I could never do that." In an instant, their compassion for what we were going through became a dagger. They made me feel isolated in a way not even the NICU itself did. They made me feel alone, separated, and placed in a category that wasn't human at a time when I was acutely aware of how fragile it is to be human. People's statements implied that there was something about me that was different from them. But I wasn't different. I was just in pain.

You could never do this? I'd think. *You could, though, because you wouldn't have a choice.* I sure didn't have a say in the matter. I got through it because I had to, not because I wanted to. The problem with "I could never do that" statements is that they excuse us from feeling the reality of what the other person is experiencing. They allow us to distance ourselves from their pain and, in doing so, shoves the other person deeper into it.

It took all the self-control I could muster in my exhausted state to nod my head and say, "Yeah, it's really hard." I hated every ounce of honor and reverence people showed me because of something that was completely out of my control. What I wanted to say was, "You think I'm not broken? You think I'm okay? You think I'm just cool with this? I can't do this either. I can't even breathe. I don't get to choose. I was forced into this, and I don't have the luxury of saying, 'I could never.' I just have to."

I didn't want to spend eight weeks in the NICU—I just had to.

The only thing I could choose was to keep getting up every day. Everything else was against my will. I didn't want to be brave. I didn't want this year of trauma on all our bodies. I just wanted to be home with my babies.

When we can't imagine ourselves in someone else's shoes, it's easier to believe there's something about that person that makes them stronger or braver than we are, and that's how they're able to endure this. We can't accept that they're like us, because that would mean we aren't safe. If it could happen to someone like us, it could happen to us—and that's a reality we don't want to ponder.

It's hard to imagine what a two-pound baby feels like until you have one on your chest. It's hard to understand the fragility of life until someone you love is hanging on by a thread. It's hard to understand how a strong faith can fall apart and be sewn back together until you've had to repair the loose threads of your own faith tapestry. So you perceive a strength in someone else that you don't think you have, and you place them on a pedestal they never wanted to be on.

"Othering" is what we do to people when we place them in a different category from us and then use that difference to separate ourselves from them. We find a million different ways to express to someone that they're *other*. We can send out the message loudly or subtly, but it comes across clearly: *You are not like me, and I am not like you.*

The othering of people who suffer happens when we elevate them onto a pedestal our theology built for them. Our theology tells us that they must be experiencing this pain because their faith is so strong or because God knew they could handle it or because they have a platform for God to shine on.

Believing that pain has a greater spiritual purpose makes it easier for us to digest. But pain isn't meant to be digested. It isn't something we're supposed to consume. We can honor someone's strength and faith without attaching it to an abstract concept of spiritual greatness. God has not called us to be spiritual masochists, trying to prove the strength of our faith through our pain. We should look at our suffering not to find what we can merit from it but to find the cure for it.

When your theology justifies suffering instead of offering a solution for it, it's simply bad theology. If you surrender to your circumstances to the point of not wanting to find a way out, you're putting yourself in a place of perpetual victimization. If you believe you're destined to endure suffering because of the holy life you're living for God, you're acting as if you don't have a Savior who came to take punishment for you.

Sometimes things happen that completely alter our lives, and there's nothing we can do to change our circumstances. We're the victims of crime, tragedy, grief, people with power, or our own choices. There are so many dangers that come with living as human beings on a broken earth. We can't undo the past. We can't control other people. We can't rewrite our decisions. There are times we can't even follow the breadcrumbs to the moment it all went wrong.

But if we believe that the gospel is true, that means hope, joy, and peace are accessible to every one of us. If Christ is the Messiah and the Son of God, then he has provided a way out for every kind of suffering we go through.

I can't tell you why something painful happened to you. I wouldn't try to give you a reason, even if you asked. I don't know. I can't tell you how you'll heal or how soon you'll feel okay again or how life will look next year or five years from now or ten years from now.

But I do know that God doesn't keep us in catastrophe as a reward for serving him. He doesn't throw us into a pit of death and say, "Rejoice and be glad that I did this to you!" Not once, in the whole story of God and his people, does he allow suffering for the sole purpose of making us earn his approval or so we can earn some kind of spiritual upgrade.

Instead, God's Word shows us the story of a God who rescues his people from their calamity (yes, even the self-induced ones) over and over again. There is no story of suffering without a redemptive arc.

- Adam and Eve got kicked out of the Garden, but he still made a way for them to live and thrive.
- God sent a flood to destroy the earth, but first he told Noah to build a boat.
- The Israelites were captured, enslaved, and abused, but he rescued them over and over again.
- God's people wandered in the desert, but he led them to the land he'd promised.
- David was chosen, then chased, and then he became the king of Israel . . . and a direct ancestor to Jesus.
- The Ninevites were going to be destroyed, but God sent Jonah to tell them to repent, and they were spared.
- Ruth and Naomi lost their husbands and their home, but God brought Boaz to take care of them.
- Job lost his family and his entire livelihood, but God restored it all.
- The thief hanging on the cross next to Jesus was convicted and executed, but Jesus told him he would be with him in heaven.
- Saul murdered people for believing in Jesus, and then he met him, got a new name, and became a pillar of the church.

Suffering will come—we know this. At some point, your heart will ache. And when that happens, your heartache will unearth what you believe about God's role in your suffering. Is he a distant observer of your pain? Did he orchestrate these circumstances to teach you something or to reward you for a job well done? Or is he actively working on your behalf to rescue you from pain while also being present with you in it?

God cannot be a good God and also be ambivalent. He cannot be redemptive and purposefully keep us in catastrophe. He cannot be just if he causes calamity and offers no way out.

Who do you believe God is?

The rest of the passage in James says that we're to consider suffering joy "because you know that the testing of your faith produces endurance. And let endurance have its full effect, so that you may be mature and complete, lacking nothing."* Paul echoes this idea in Romans: "We also boast in our afflictions, because we know that affliction produces endurance, endurance produces proven character, and proven character produces hope."†

James and Paul say the same thing about suffering: we rejoice, we boast, we consider it joy . . . *because we know*. We can rejoice while we're hurting because we know something about the cure. We know something about what happens here on earth and what's waiting for us in the Kingdom of God. *We know something.*[1]

The mysteries of God frustrate us when we're only longing for the answer to why we're suffering, how long we'll suffer, and when we'll be rescued. But those same mysteries are a comfort because we know there's something bigger at work. We might not be able to see what goes on beyond the veil separating heaven from earth, but we know something about the God who rules them.

Even in our greatest pain, we have the gift of hope. This enables

---

* *James 1:3-4,* CSB
† *Romans 5:3-4,* CSB

us to "not focus on what is seen, but on what is unseen. For what is seen is temporary, but what is unseen is eternal."* We live in a kingdom we can see and touch and taste, but we know there is an invisible Kingdom that lies just beyond the veil, and in that coming Kingdom, all that is wrong will be made right. Our faith emboldens us to hope.

The joy that we're to consider isn't found in our heartbreak; it's found in knowing there's something beyond the suffering. There's an "after" for us to look forward to. The dark nights we endure are an invitation to strengthen our faith. The strength we gain produces an endurance in us that helps us survive the next hard thing.

The joy we're to consider is found in the comfort we receive in our heartache. We receive that comfort from the throne room of heaven— a comfort that's rich with knowledge,

> The joy that we're to consider isn't found in our heartbreak; it's found in knowing there's something beyond the suffering.

trust, hope, and love. It carries with it depth and levity that can only come from knowing that even in our worst-case scenario, we are held and loved by a God who is good and kind and faithful. And when we internalize that comfort ourselves, we're also able to comfort others in their suffering.†

❋

One of the church's favorite verses on suffering is Psalm 30:11: "You turned my lament into dancing; you removed my sackcloth and clothed me with gladness" (CSB). This idea of mourning being exchanged for dancing has been the inspiration for some of the most heartfelt Christian art and worship. It's a beautiful prayer to

---

* *2 Corinthians 4:18*, CSB
† *2 Corinthians 1:3-7*

cry out when we're hurting and to sing out when we're past the hurt, looking back on what God has done.

But like many of our favorite verses, these words can be twisted in ways that invite us to dismiss our humanity and make us feel bad if we can't move straight to dancing. If God can turn our mourning into dancing and we're still sad, it must mean there is a lack of faith on our part. It's the same idea as "trading my sorrows" for "the joy of the Lord," as one of the popular songs from my Christian youth group days said.

He doesn't exchange our mourning; he transforms it.

According to Psalm 30:11, there's an exchange that should happen. But what if I gave God my sorrow, and I'm still covered in the ashes of grief? If that exchange doesn't happen immediately, it must mean I've done something wrong.

When Scripture talks about God turning our mourning into dancing, it isn't about trading a bad thing for a good thing. It isn't a transaction that requires us to hand over our grief in return for God's joy. He doesn't exchange our mourning; he transforms it. If you've ever held grief, you know that mourning never ends—at least not in this life. There's no moving on—we just learn to move with it. In time, and by God's grace, we learn to move our bodies again. We remember our joy. We learn to live with our heartbreak, and eventually we learn to dance with it.

The hope we have in Christ allows us to laugh while we're grieving and dance while we're suffering. Joy isn't just waiting for us when we're all healed up and "over it." There are some heartbreaks that never fully leave us.

That psalm doesn't say, "You take away the reason I was mourning in the first place." The thing that hurt you will always be the thing that hurt you, but you won't always hurt in the same way. You'll change. You'll grow. You'll make room for dancing. You'll make room for joy. There are no guarantees that circumstances will get better. The only sure thing we have is that Jesus will be with us in the pain and will be our joy in spite of it.

I think that's something worth dancing about, don't you?

Suffering in itself doesn't mark us as special or distinguish us in any way. But the *way* we suffer does. We endure hardship not as people who have nothing to look forward to but as people with *everything* to look forward to. We know that from here, it only gets better, even if the pain stays with us. We can maintain joy because our joy isn't sourced in our circumstances. Things don't have to be perfect and light and easy for us to have true, contagious joy.

There are times when you feel parched. You get so used to being sad that you forget whether you've ever been happy. It's hard to remember joy you aren't sure you've ever experienced. So how is it possible for joy and grief to exist together?

It's possible because there are oceans within you. You are human, but you aren't simple. You're a beautifully complex creation of a God who himself is beautifully complex. The thirteenth-century poet Rumi wrote, "You are not a drop in the ocean, you are the ocean in a drop." Just like the ocean, you're capable of holding and releasing so much more than you can imagine, because you were created that way. God, who is full of mystery, made you to reflect his mystery. A dynamic God made you capable of being dynamic. Imagine that!

Your joy isn't dependent on your circumstances or the absence of negative feelings. Your anger and sorrow can coexist with joy. That's how supernatural the joy within you is. It doesn't need you to do anything or be anything other than *his*. You don't need to exchange one feeling for another—you can hold them all. You contain oceans, after all.

We have a Savior who is good. He invites us to set down the heavy heartache we carry, and he doesn't ask us to pick it up again.

He carries our burdens for us, and he strengthens us, as the family of God, to carry burdens for each other as well.

We don't need hardship to tell us where we stand with God. He has already told us. We're his children, and we're loved and beloved by him. He doesn't take a measuring stick to our lives and decide whether we've had our fair share of trials and tribulations. He's not standing next to our beds with a bucket of lice to "reward" us for doing well. It's his goodness and mercy that will follow you all the days of your life,* not calamity and pain (or bugs!).

❋

After seven weeks in the NICU for Chloe and eight weeks for Lydia, we were finally able to bring them home. At that point, we didn't know what their future would look like. We weren't sure if their medical conditions would worsen. We were just so thankful they were alive that we didn't think to ask for more than that.

We'd factored in God's power, but we hadn't accounted for his extravagance.

A few weeks after the girls came home, we drove to Boston Children's Hospital for a consultation with the neurosurgeon. Our miraculous Baby B, Lydia, had two conditions: hydrocephalus and ventriculomegaly. She had extra fluid on her brain, causing pressure to build in her brain and enlarging her ventricles.

The fluid had been present from the time I was nineteen weeks pregnant, and the doctors had been tracking her fluid, ventricle size, and head growth ever since. The fluid buildup had never been significant enough to require immediate treatment, but it was enough of a concern that we began a long-term relationship with

---

Psalm 23:6

the neurology departments at both our local hospital and Boston Children's. When we brought Lydia home, it was with the understanding that she might need a shunt to drain the fluid from her brain. When we drove to Boston that day, we were expecting to make an appointment to have surgery.

That's not what happened.

When we got to the hospital, Lydia and I were led to the MRI machine. I lay on top of her, holding her little chin still while the spaceship-like MRI machine spun around us.

Afterward, as we waited to be called in to review the results, Zach and I wondered if they'd want to do the surgery that day. We talked about the logistics—if we'd need to stay the night, who would watch the older kids, and how soon we'd have to return for a post-op follow-up.

When the doctor called us back, he casually sat down on a stool (a little *too* casually), and we exchanged small talk for a few minutes. I was bouncing my foot frantically but trying to remain cool and calm because *he* was cool and calm.

He must have noticed that my foot was about to detach from my ankle because he quickly changed the course of the conversation. He took a breath and said the only words I remember from that appointment: "There is no hydrocephalus present."

I'm sure he said other things, but all Zach and I heard was ringing in our ears. This time it was a good ringing—the kind of ringing that happens when you're in a stadium full of people cheering. After the doctor was done saying whatever else he said, he walked out of the room and Zach and I looked at each other—mouths open, eyes wide—and burst into tears.

Both of us started to speak and then lost our words before we could form a sentence. The conversation involved a lot of "Did he—?" "What does that—?" "Is she—?" "Are we—?" and "I can't—"

We shook our heads and laughed like we hadn't laughed in a really long time. In the euphoria of the moment, I watched Zach's eyes brighten. It was like watching the shadows of an early morning disappear as the sun comes up. He stepped into the light and breathed.

We had prepared ourselves for every possible medical outcome. We were ready to love a medically complicated child, and we'd braced ourselves for whatever needs her condition would bring.

We hadn't prepared for . . . nothing. For her to be healed in full. It was too good to be true, and yet it was real. I tried to rationalize what the doctor had just told us. I tried to minimize it. But there was no reasoning my way out of this miracle. The only thing we could do was bask in it.

What a mercy. What a joy.

God didn't have to do that. We still would have believed. We'd agreed on his goodness regardless of the outcome. We would have still lived our lives surrendered to him and committed to the Kingdom of God. At least, I hope we would have.

He didn't have to, but he did. A miracle like this wasn't on our radar. Yet he chose to display his glory and his goodness in a way we didn't even imagine. After finding his goodness for so long in the "he didn't," it was momentously joyful to experience it in the "he did."

The joy in the heart of a believer is more than just an emotion we feel in response to the good things around us. It isn't being excited about suffering because it proves our good standing with God. And it isn't something we fabricate to deny our sorrow and win some kind of "suffering Christian" award.

The joy in our spirits is a gift from the Creator. It's a supernatural gladness that locks hands with our grief. Joy empowers us to know the fullness of who God is and the rich love that's available to us through our connection with him and the love we receive from the family of God.

That's why we can have joy in mourning. That's the reason we can dance—not because we're forced to, but because it's the natural response to the hope we have in Christ. Our joy comes in knowing there's more to this life and there's more after it.

I'll dance to that.

THE DISTORTION:

Suffering is proof that
I am in the will of God.

✳

THE SHIFT:

Jesus came to bear my suffering for me,
not reward me with it for a job well done.

9

The Sacredness of Shared Pain

Our brain works best when we have people who
are genuinely glad to be with us.

CHRIS COURSEY

I OPENED INSTAGRAM ONE DAY and read a message from someone I
didn't know. I realized right away that the contents of the message
were clearly meant for someone else. Every now and then, someone will try to send one of my posts to a friend and accidentally
send me a message instead. I don't know if it's the weird layout of
the options or a technological Freudian slip, but it's not the first
time this has happened.

The person wrote, "I just don't understand, why *her*? She's not
even thankful for what she has."

The message echoed what other people had expressed to me
in less direct ways. Why was I still hurting when we'd gotten what
we prayed for? As they peered through the window of my life, they
saw that my babies were healthy and happy, and they interpreted
my emotional pain as ingratitude.

The question stung. Would you ask someone who had surgery why their incision still hurt?

But this was something I wrestled with too. I should just be thankful. I had five kids. My prayers had been answered. What right did I have to be sad?

There were days after we'd brought the girls home from the hospital when I'd be crying on my bed, biting my blanket so no one would hear me. I'd beat myself up with the same words that crossed the minds of those who criticized my response to my suffering. *Just be thankful. Why are you so weak? You got what you asked for, so shut up, you ungrateful, selfish mess.*

In my darkest moments, the harshest comments other people spoke to me became my inner monologue. But what other people observed revealed more about what was in their hearts than what was actually true about me. I wasn't ungrateful; I was just injured.

The way we judge others when they suffer and navigate difficult circumstances reveals a lot about us. We all do it. We observe pain and cast judgment about the person feeling it.

We quickly try to make sense of their experience by asking a few qualifying questions. *Did they do something to bring this on themselves? How long has it been since this happened? Should they be over it by now? Are they getting bitter? Have they taken this to Jesus? Are they truly putting their faith in Jesus? Are they suffering well?* If we can find a loophole in their suffering, we can excuse ourselves from entering their pain and showing them compassion.

※

When I was a teenager, I attended a large church with a friend whose dad was the pastor. One week during the worship service, my friend elbowed me and pointed to the aisle. An usher, dressed in a suit and holding a finger to his earpiece, walked to the front row. He went up to a man whose arms were raised in worship and tapped him on the shoulder. The usher smiled and bent down to whisper something in the man's ear.

The man nodded his head and stood up, and then the usher motioned for him to step into the aisle. They walked to the back of the sanctuary together, and the usher directed the man to the last row.

My friend whispered, "That's because he's homeless. The cameras only show the people in the first couple of rows, and people might not feel safe coming to our church if they see homeless people in the front row."

Teenagers often create their own interpretations of events, but pastors' kids tend to know a lot about what goes on in their churches. I don't know if that's really the reason the usher escorted the man to the back, but I'll never forget the look on the man's face. It didn't matter that the usher was kind, that he smiled, or that he was gentle. The maybe-homeless man was embarrassed.

I kept glancing back at him throughout the service. He never raised his hands again. He hung his head lower and lower until he eventually got up and walked out.

This man's suffering brought shame to the community he was worshiping with. The usher did exactly what James said not to do: "If someone comes into your meeting wearing a gold ring and dressed in fine clothes, and a poor person dressed in filthy clothes also comes in, if you look with favor on the one wearing the fine clothes and say, 'Sit here in a good place,' and yet you say to the poor person, 'Stand over there,' or 'Sit here on the floor by my footstool,' haven't you made distinctions among yourselves and become judges with evil thoughts?"*

* *James 2:2-4,* CSB

Christianity presents a radical departure from the world's economy and system of importance. There is no spiritual elevation based on rich or poor, or on suffering or lack of it. There's no evaluation system to determine someone's worth or how they're to be treated. We're all equal. We're one body. When one suffers, we all suffer.

Scripture is dripping with the call to serve each other, love each other, carry each other, encourage each other, and treat each other the way Christ has treated us. This is what separated Christianity from the other faiths that were growing in popularity at the time the Gospels were written. It wasn't the belief in one God (there were other monotheistic religions at the time); it wasn't the belief in a resurrected God (there were other religions that believed their god died and rose again); it wasn't even the miracles that took place (there were other "miracles" at the hands of other gods).[1] It wasn't any of that. It was the way Christians treated each other and cared for those who were suffering.

Cyprian was a Christian bishop at the time of the Plague of Cyprian (which was unfortunately named after him, simply because he documented it). The plague lasted for roughly a decade (249–262 AD), and it was a brutal one, marked by fatigue, fever, deafness, blindness, hemorrhaging, bloody stools, lesions on the throat, and infections in the fingers and toes. It was an agonizing sickness that led to an agonizing death.

The death toll each *day* was in the thousands. Because the sickness meant an inevitable death sentence, when a person became infected and started to show symptoms, they were removed from their house and placed outside the city walls to die alone.

Christians, however, responded differently. Their response was so radical that it led to the massive growth of Christianity throughout the Roman Empire. Cyprian's writings tell us that Christians neither left the cities where the plague was spreading nor abandoned their loved ones when they got sick. They cared for the sick and faced the inevitability of their deaths with peace, trusting that there was life in heaven waiting for them.[2]

Dionysius, a fellow bishop at the time of Cyprian, wrote that most people "pushed the sufferers away and fled from their dearest, throwing them into the roads before they were dead." Meanwhile, "most of our brother-Christians showed unbounded love and loyalty, never sparing themselves and thinking only of each other. Heedless of the danger, they took charge of the sick, attending to their every need and ministering to them in Christ, and with them departed this life serenely happy."[3]

The way Christians cared for the sick and the dying during the plagues led to the development of hospitals and laid the foundation for modern medicine as we know it. Their posture toward meeting the needs of others, regardless of what it cost them, has caused historians to speculate that historically, the Christian response to sickness and suffering was the most effective method of spreading the message of Christ.

Nurture is built into our Christian ethics, yet today it seems all but lost. Imagine what Christians could do for the world of trauma and mental health if we nurtured the suffering the way we nurtured the sick. Our response to suffering, in any context, shouldn't look like the world's, unless the world's response looks like Jesus'—full of compassion, kindness, and empathy, regardless of how that suffering came into the person's life.

Yet the church has a reputation for being stingy with our compassion. Sure, compassion doesn't come easily. And personality wise, some people are naturally wired to be concerned for others while others tend to lean more toward cynicism. As a society, we value self-preservation and are selective about who we'll offer our compassion to.

Have you ever looked at someone else's heartache and thought, *Did they bring this on themselves somehow?* If so, that's a pretty clear sign that you've been jaded by the world's cynicism. Regardless of the choices someone may or may not have made, we never have a reason to withhold compassion from someone who's in pain.

When someone has experienced unthinkable heartache, we tend to be wary about getting too close to them. If we deem their decisions reckless or wrong, we keep them at a distance, lest they (or other people) think we're supporting their choices. We worry that our kindness will only enable them, and we think that "tough love" will bring them out of the darkness. We narrow our eyes and think, *What's the other side of this story? They must have done something to deserve this.*

While we were navigating our crisis pregnancy, I would often get anxious that people were wondering those things about us. Every time someone offered advice on how to "heal my placenta" with different herbal remedies and diets, I'd wonder if it was a passive-aggressive accusation that our daughters' problems were my fault. My past experience with being accused of bringing on my own suffering had made me defensive and cautious about even the most well-meaning advice and help.

Maybe part of the problem is that we have a tendency to make other people's suffering about *us*. We act like we're entitled to the whole story before we offer our compassion. But doesn't God's Word compel us toward action, not reservation?

Let's imagine for a minute that someone *did* do something to deserve their heartache. What are the qualifications for compassion? Who gets to determine where the line is? We have imaginary rules that say someone can do all *these things* and be worthy of compassion, but if they do anything past this line, we don't owe it to them. Who makes the line? And why does crossing it give us permission to withhold our compassion?

Here's the thing: God knows everything about *us*, and he's still kind to us.

There have been plenty of times that my suffering was brought on by my own stupid, selfish decisions. And in the middle of those consequences, God was still kind to me. His grace is big enough to cover our dumb decisions. Grace and compassion aren't reserved for times when our pain is caused by something beyond our control. Even when we're the architects of our own suffering, his grace is available and accessible to us. He is compassionate, even in his discipline.

> Compassion will never be the reason someone keeps making mistakes.

I think we're sometimes afraid that if we're too gracious to people, no lessons will be learned—as if someone's learning curve depends on our response to their pain. It's the "tough love" approach that is tough but isn't really so much love. We take it upon ourselves to be instructors of difficult life lessons when what we're called to be is a loving friend. Sometimes tough love can be a beneficial wake-up call, but most of the time it's the knife in a gaping wound that needs care.

If everyone keeps giving hurting people tough love, who will equip them with what they need to overcome? Compassion will never be the reason someone keeps making mistakes. It *could*, however, be the thing that stops the cycle.

✳

When we were healing from our church trauma, I was talking to a woman I'd just met about what happened.* It's a painful story to

---

* This woman has since become a close friend and ministry partner to my husband and me, and she is one of the endorsers of this book. Hi, Toni!

tell—one that requires a lot of time and a bit of backstory. When I tell it, I often feel myself getting defensive, as if I have to prove that my hurt was justified. It can feel really dehumanizing to have to defend your wounds.

As I was talking, I could tell she was getting uncomfortable. Her eyebrows furrowed, and I assumed she was evaluating the situation to determine whether I was worthy of her empathy. I reached the end of the story, and she didn't say a word. She just sat there, staring, her eyebrows still in a worried expression.

Her silence made me uneasy, so I tried to wrap things up with a bow. "But it's okay now!" I told her. "We wouldn't be where we are if that hadn't happened, so it's fine. God is good." Inside I was thinking, *Please don't dismiss me. Please don't say something about how I deserved it. This really, really hurt.*

She just shook her head. "You don't have to do that." She took a long pause and then said, "I just want to grieve with you for a minute."

The pain I'd been choking back for what seemed like forever caught in my throat. I was speechless. Surprised by compassion. She gave me a gift no one else had given me yet. With her gift of compassion, she freed me.

Our friends and family had given us solidarity and anger (both of which were priceless for our hurting hearts), but in that moment I learned that I also needed a tender touch. I needed someone to share my burden and carry my grief, even if it was just for the moment.

I needed a hug. I needed someone to get close to me and not worry if my "suffering germs" would rub off on them. I didn't need tough love—I just needed love. Her willingness to share a grief that wasn't hers to carry gave me the relief I needed to help to heal those parts that were still broken.

It's hard to give what you haven't been given. Compassion can be learned, sure, but when it has been given freely to you, you can give it to others too. That's what happened for me. Her gentle sadness over our tragedy didn't make me want to stay sad and angry and bitter; it made me want to let go and move on and do for others what she'd just done for me.

Compassion isn't enabling—it's empowering. As believers, we should have a gut reaction of compassion to suffering of any kind, without having to vet the source first.

I think part of the reason this interaction impacted me so much is because I'd never encountered that kind of compassion before. When the pain of what happened at our church was still raw, I didn't really know how to talk about it. I was walking around with an open wound, bleeding out and disoriented from shock and pain. I was broken and hurting in a way I couldn't put into words, so I just talked. And talked. And talked. It was the only thing I could talk about.

I'm sure people were thinking, *When is she gonna get over this?*

My hurt came up in almost every conversation. It consumed my mind, so it consumed my conversations. But in that continual conversation I kept having with everyone, I started noticing how people's responses changed the further I unpacked the story.

First their response was shock. They couldn't believe the pastor had said what he'd said, the board had done what they'd done, the people had treated us the way they'd treated us. It was too awful, too unexpected. Nobody who loved us could understand why people who loved Jesus would treat us like that.

As they processed what I'd told them, they'd come back to the conversation wondering if it had happened the way we described it. Was there more to the story? Could we think of anything we'd done to bring this on ourselves? What was the pastor's side of the story? Maybe he went about it the wrong way, but were his actions really *wrong*?

Then they moved to concern for us—but not concern for our healing or health, and not concern that we felt loved and supported. Rather, they were concerned that our pain would drive us to deconstruct our faith or walk away from our calling to be in full-time ministry. Even some of my closest friends stepped back and stopped checking in with me.

Other friends and family would tell me I was coming across bitter and angry, and I would turn people away from the church if I didn't stop being so open about my pain. "Wait until you're healed to talk about it," they told me.

I learned that my pain was acceptable for a certain period of time, and then it became too uncomfortable for other people. The intensity of our emotions was understandable when we were standing in the wake of massive hurt and betrayal, but when others deemed that the waters should have settled, our pain became a liability.

People I loved and who loved me refused to step into my pain with me, to feel it with me, to ask me questions about it, to try to understand it. Instead, they stood on the outside, offering their observations and calling me to come to them instead of getting into the murky waters with me. For years, I waded through the mud on my own because the church has a way of putting a time limit on compassion. Once we decide it's time for people to be "over it," we withdraw our sensitivity to their pain. The statute of limitations is up—it's time to move on.

Even though I'm on the other side of healing now and I'm still in loving relationships with those people, I look back on that time with so much sadness. It's isolating to have friends look at you like you're a risk to their reputation. Like they can't share that they're connected to you, lest other people think they condone the thoughts and doubts you're wrestling with as you heal from trauma.

I know what it's like to be the messy friend, the messy sibling, the messy daughter. I know what it's like to sit at a table with people you've known your entire life and be cut off from the conversation because your hurt has made your perspective too biased to be valued.

I know what it's like to have people dismiss your pain and micromanage your response to it. I know what it's like to have someone you're looking to for support put their hand in your face and tell you to let your husband do the talking.

I know what it's like when the family of God abandons you when you need them most—not because you did something wrong, but because you aren't processing your pain in a way that has been preapproved by some unspoken charter of Christian pain management.

So this is my public service announcement: there is no sin in messy pain management. The wisest thing we can do is process our trauma, not hold it in. We learn wisdom as we grow and mature in our walk with Christ. It isn't something we obtain the moment we start following Jesus.

Sometimes processing pain is messy and uncomfortable and even inappropriate. You'll probably say things you wouldn't say on the other side of healing, wherever that mythical "other side" is. You might look back on it five years later with regret and embarrassment. You might need to dish out some humble apologies. But messy isn't the same as sinful. And messy never disqualifies you from being worthy of love, compassion, and understanding from the family of God.

Someone else's pain isn't ours to manage or judge; it's ours to hold for our brothers and sisters. Stepping into a person's pain and truly being with them in it requires that we die

Messy never disqualifies you from being worthy of love, compassion, and understanding from the family of God.

to ourselves—something that God's Word tells us to do over and over again. It means that we willingly step into someone else's pain, knowing we'll get some of their "ick" on us. Other people may look at us and may see our compassion as a stamp of approval. They might give us serious side-eye or take us aside after church to lovingly correct us and warn us about the company we keep.

Kind of like people did with Jesus, right?

If we're going to do the work of the Kingdom of God, we don't get to decide who is worthy of our compassion and who isn't. When we carry the cross of Christ, we choose to carry whatever pain and suffering come with it. If we die to self, we don't get to pick and choose what parts of ourselves we die to. We can't compartmentalize what we allow Christ to transform. Choosing Christ means repeatedly choosing him, even when doing so comes at great cost.

And it will. When we die to self, we put our pride to death over and over again. When we don't, the cost is a lack of compassion and love toward people who are in pain.

I'm so thankful Jesus doesn't wait to see where we're going with our doubts and our pain before he engages with us. He doesn't abandon us in our wanderings. He doesn't leave us pacing empty rooms as we try to figure out the complex nuances of faith and hardship. If Jesus doesn't do that to us, why do we do it to each other? Who are we to look down on anyone else and decide whether they're worthy of our compassion?

As Zach and I were processing the pain of our church experience, we found a community of people who had been hurt in a similar way. The solution they offered was togetherness. They just wanted to be with us. They wrapped their arms around us—messy pain and doubts and all—and sat with us in it.

They didn't rush us through the process. They didn't tell us what to believe. They didn't panic about our doubts. They didn't tell us what we should or shouldn't do. They didn't warn us of the dangers of bitterness.

They just came alongside us as we bled out. They changed our bandages, stitched us up when they could, and cared for us until we could tend to our own wounds. They were the hands and feet of Christ to us at a time when we were reevaluating what we believed about the family of God. They showed us who Jesus really is, and in doing so, helped us to rebuild the framework of our faith.

❋

When we're judgmental of others, it's typically because we're craving a sense of control. If we can have an airtight sense of what's right and what's wrong, we won't be touched by someone else's crisis. We try to pin down what caused their pain in an attempt to make sure the same thing won't happen to us. Instead of facing the discomfort of admitting that we don't know the answer, we jump to overconfidence in what we *think* we know.

Our standoffish response to other people's pain reveals where we don't trust God with our image and reputation. It exposes our selfish concern that being too close to someone else's mess will harm us in ways that God can't redeem, protect, or manage. It reveals that we value our image, our time, our finances, or our energy over sitting with someone in their pain. It reveals aspects of our faith that are theoretical only.

When people say things like "The church didn't hurt you—people did!" they're communicating, "This isn't my fault, so this isn't my responsibility." But it is your responsibility. When one of us hurts, we all hurt.

There's a reason the New Testament writers describe the family of God as a body.* God was creative in his design of the human body. In order to function properly, all the parts of the body need the whole and the whole needs all the parts. The church is designed by the same Creator, and it needs every part to function the way God intended it to.

In *Designed to Heal*, Jennie McLaurin and Cymbeline Culiat use their medical and scientific backgrounds to make in-depth parallels between the way the human body heals from a wound and the way the Christian body is made to heal. In each chapter, they describe how the body of believers can respond to nonphysical wounds the same way first responders and medical teams respond to a physically injured person.

There are different responses for different wounds, but each person has a vital role in the healing process. Some people are like the body's inflammatory response—they're the ones who help get rid of whatever is preventing the body from healing. They are reactive and defensive—a crucial immediate response to an injury. Then there are those who stop the bleeding. They apply "positive pressure with kindness." They're a peaceful presence, offering casseroles and lawn mowing. The first responders to a wound don't offer advice or trite Christian platitudes; they simply respond to the injury.[4]

Do you know what happens in your brain when you make eye contact with someone who's happy to see you? Let's do a little exercise. Picture yourself walking into a room. When you look at who's there, you see every person who has ever made you feel safe and happy. As you walk into the room, they look up and notice

* 1 Corinthians 12:12-26

you. How do they respond? Do they smile? Do they get up and walk toward you? Do they give you a hug? What do they say?

I picture myself walking into my grandmother's living room. When I walk in, Nana wipes her hands on her apron (because she was in the kitchen making a peach cobbler for me). She smiles, gives me a hug, and welcomes me in. It's always a quick hug, though. Nana doesn't linger—she has things to do. I follow her into the kitchen, where my cousins and siblings are sitting at the table.

They jump and yell, "Yay! You're here!" and take turns hugging me. They immediately tell me something ridiculous someone said before I got there. We laugh, grab forks, and dig into the cobbler.

When I think of people who are glad to be with me no matter what I'm going through, I think of them. These are my low-pressure relationships. I don't have to put on a show or hide any part of me. They're just happy I'm there.

The people who are happy to be with us don't wait until they see what's in the bags we're dragging behind us. They immediately jump up to greet us and welcome us into their space. They just smile and let us in.

Joy lights up the relational circuits of your brain that make con-

> We don't have to understand someone's pain to make room for it.

nection and trust possible.[5] When you're safe, you can face the dark with courage, knowing that you aren't alone and that you don't have to hurry through it. After looking each demon in the face, you can come up for air, trusting that these people are happy to see you, no matter how haggard you are when you surface.

We don't have to understand someone's pain to make room for it. We don't have to know what someone else is carrying to decide whether their emotional state is justified. We can just be glad that they're with us and let them know that they're safe as they are, baggage and all.

Heartbreak leaves you wondering if you're broken, if you've been forgotten, if God has abandoned and rejected you. You start avoiding the sharp elbows of well-meaning brothers and sisters in Christ and start looking for a soft, grace-filled place to land and rest. Not so you can run from truth or entertain the heresy you've been itching to try out, but so you can breathe.

When pain derails your life, you no longer find peace in the hard edges of certainty. Instead, you find comfort in the presence of the God who is with us. In those moments, you give up trying to make your pain fit neatly inside a particular framework. You just want to know that you aren't alone.

There's comfort in lament, in songs written in minor keys, and in the darker shades of paint.

There is transformational, healing power in knowing that you aren't the only one who has held the pain you're holding. There's hope in seeing someone who has ached the way you've ached—and survived. There's comfort in lament, in songs written in minor keys, and in the darker shades of paint. You are drawn to those things not because you want to feed your sadness but because they mirror where you find yourself. When you see a painting that visualizes an emotion you have, or when you hear a song that puts words to something you haven't been able to explain, or when you read words that make you feel understood, you are able to see yourself and your pain a little more clearly.

We are created in the image of God, so when we see ourselves, we see the image of God reflected back to us. When we perceive this reflection as broken or wasted, it makes us uncomfortable. Pain doesn't feel like anything holy.

But maybe it's easier to see the sacredness of it when we realize we're in good company. The pain we've experienced has been felt by all the heroes of the faith across the ages.

It's a pain that's familiar to God himself. He knows heartbreak, agony, disappointment, anger, and grief. Lament is a sacred part of our faith—one we can welcome and embrace. There's no virtue in rushing ourselves—or others—past it. Lamenting what we've lost isn't a sad, unfortunate human response to suffering; it's a beautiful, healing one.

When we see someone suffering, we can focus on sin. We can focus on blame. We can focus on mess. Or we can observe the heart of Christ for those who are suffering and bear witness to their pain, even if it costs us something.

If we allow ourselves and each other to engage with every crack made by pain, we have the opportunity to see and know God in ways we haven't before. When we stop trying to rush people past lament and urging them to "move on," whatever that means, we allow them to experience the faith building that can happen when we're hurting. When we don't rush someone's pain and instead experience it with them, we are communicating the gospel message that we love them—not out of obligation, but because we are glad to be together, no matter what.

Grab a fork, and dive into the cobbler.

THE DISTORTION:
The reason someone is suffering and
their response to that suffering determines
the level of compassion they deserve.

✳

THE SHIFT:
Compassion, given freely and without restriction,
reflects the heart of the Father to those who are
hurting, regardless of how that pain happened.

10

The Glory around Us

Jesus doesn't give an explanation for the pain and sorrow of the world. He comes where the pain is most acute and takes it upon himself. Jesus doesn't explain why there is suffering, illness, and death in the world. He brings healing and hope. He doesn't allow the problem of evil to be the subject of a seminar. He allows evil to do its worst to him. He exhausts it, drains its power, and emerges with new life.

N. T. WRIGHT

EVERYTHING THAT HAD HAPPENED over the past year started to metabolize in my body after we brought Chloe and Lydia home from the hospital. They were born at the beginning of May, and they were released from the hospital at the end of June. We bought a house in mid-September. And just as the first snow was falling and all New England began to hibernate, I started to feel the effects of the trauma we'd just walked through.

It didn't happen all at once. In some ways that might have been easier—just hit me really hard one time, I'll heal, and it'll be over. Instead, the breaking happened with a million little taps on the glass. A million little fractures in my heart.

I was hurting so deeply, and I felt so much guilt for hurting when every day I held two living, breathing miracles in my arms.

How could I feel so broken? How could I be so sad? I had everything I'd asked for and more, and yet I was falling apart.

Grief would randomly fall on top of me like a weight, suffocating me and making me feel like this was my fault. *You're only happy when you're sad. When there's no crisis, you make up problems. You have your babies, you have your health, you have a beautiful home, and you don't deserve any of it.*

As each day passed, all the defenses I'd built to protect myself in the middle of the crisis started to shatter. The smallest things became triggers that sent me into spirals of shame, anger, and despair.

One night, Zach was reading a book out loud to the kids. He'd grabbed it off the shelf and started reading, not realizing this book was a trigger for me. It was the book I'd read to the girls every day when they were in the NICU.

When he started reading in his soft-spoken, monotone voice, it was as if someone were shoving razor blades under my skin. I was so angry. How could he do this to me?

I jumped off the couch and started manically cleaning the living room and the kitchen, slamming every cabinet, dish, and chair I could find. He didn't get it. The longer he read, the more my anger surfaced.

Why didn't I tell him to stop? He would have. Why didn't I leave the room? I could have.

I don't know.

All I know is that poor man received the most confusing, nasty earful for reading a book to our kids. It wasn't his fault. But it wasn't mine either.

We were brushing up against trauma that until that moment didn't have a target.

As the year progressed, I watched my family move on from our trauma. Zach and the kids went back to their routines, and so did my extended family and friends. Everyone was relieved that the girls were okay, and for them, that's where the trauma stopped. No one had anything to worry about anymore.

But I hadn't processed any of it when I was living it. I had internalized my fears and sheltered my children from knowing anything was wrong. I'd shouldered the weight of every scan, every blood draw, every blood pressure check, every heartbeat check, every worried expression on the face of each doctor and nurse who looked at our ultrasounds.

I carried it all on my own. Not because I wanted to—I wasn't being some martyr of a mother. I just drank the cup that was given to me and hoped for the best.

So while everyone else got to move forward with relief and joy, I had to unpack what I'd been carrying. I had to process what I hadn't been able to process in the moment because I was trying to survive. Once our lives slowed down, my body and my mind allowed me the space to actually *feel* what we'd gone through.

I had to process all the stages of grief, even though from the outside, it didn't seem like I had anything to grieve. But there was so much.

I had to walk through the anger of everything that had happened and the grief of all that I'd lost: time with my children, a normal pregnancy, a normal childbirth, the person I was before that first scan. I had to process all the what-ifs that came with having to make impossible choices about my daughters' lives. I hadn't allowed myself to think about worst-case scenarios when we were in the middle of it. But now I had all the time in the world, and the what-ifs came flooding into my mind.

I had to revisit the anxiety I felt with their diagnosis and the roller coaster of the prognosis that followed.

I had to grieve not being able to see my daughters for hours after they were born and not being able to hold them for days. I had to allow myself to be angry that I spent my postpartum period recovering from surgery in a NICU while my babies lay in plastic beds beside me instead of warm in bed, snuggled up with me. I had to process the frustration and exhaustion of having to pump breast milk instead of feeding my babies from my chest, and grieve the loss of that bonding.

I had to admit to myself that my connection with my older kids was broken and changed after being separated from them not just physically but emotionally as well. In my desire to protect them from experiencing fear and trauma, I hid myself from them. We lost something in that season that we can't get back.

I had to grieve the memories of that year that I'll never remember because the effects of the trauma made me forget so much. I had to face all the fear I compartmentalized in the thick of things. I had to replay the sounds of the NICU, the fear when the girls' heart monitors went off and flashed red, the sight of nurses running over and stimulating their backs to remind them to breathe.

I was reliving the entire year in my head and my heart, while also functioning as a wife and a mother in a world that had the nerve to keep moving forward.

Everyone moved on except me. I was still in the doctor's office. I was still in the hospital room. I was still in surgery. I was still in the NICU. The world around me was moving at hyper speed, and I was trying to catch up.

I needed to hold each moment and look at it, feel it, experience it, and grieve before I could move forward with it. I had to give myself permission to not be okay, even though our girls were.

God did an incredibly kind and gracious thing in sparing our daughters' lives. I've asked him many times, *If the story was always going to end up good, why did it have to hurt so bad? Why does it still have to hurt? If they were always going to be okay, why did I have to bleed for it?*

One of the narratives I've heard more than once and fought hard against is that I was a brave mother warrior, fighting doctors who were trying to kill my baby. Some people have this image of me standing on a tall pillar of faith, trusting my daughters' lives into the hands of God and enduring this trial while barely breaking a sweat.

I hate this narrative. It paints me in a light that isn't real with a strength I didn't feel. You think I didn't break a sweat? You think because I'm standing that I'm not broken?

I am powdered shards of glass.

I am bleeding onto the pages of this book.

My life has been soaked by the tears of my broken heart.

I'm broken. I will always be someone who's been broken.

That's not to say it's bad. It isn't bad to be broken. But the breaking is brutal, isn't it? It doesn't feel like a metaphor. It feels like being snapped in half over and over again.

There's beauty in the breaking. Not in a melancholy, sadistic "Look at how beautifully I'm suffering" kind of way. And not just once the broken pieces have been redeemed and rebuilt. There's beauty in the breaking itself. And there's beauty because of it.

Sometimes you aren't strong. Sometimes the hard thing breaks you. Sometimes you break into such tiny pieces that you can never rebuild yourself exactly the same. Sometimes the pain makes you unrecognizable.

But healing doesn't happen when every broken piece is lined up perfectly in the right place and seamlessly glued back together. Healing happens when you look at the broken pieces and accept that there will always be pieces that are broken, no matter how expertly they've been repaired. You can let the pieces be what they are and move forward to whatever version of you is left as you heal into someone new.

Strength isn't in your ability to not break; it's in walking forward, having been broken.

Not long ago I heard Ann Voskamp speak at the C. S. Lewis festival in Petoskey, Michigan. During her talk, she told us about her father and how her friend sent her a gift to honor the anniversary of his death.

Strength isn't in your ability to not break; it's in walking forward, having been broken.

Ann pulled a beautiful porcelain bowl out of a box. She held it up to the light and showed us how the bowl had been broken and repaired using a Japanese art called *kintsugi*. In this process, the broken pieces of the bowl are glued back together using bright gold. The result is a dish that has obviously been broken but has just as obviously been repaired.

The art is not in concealing the breaks but highlighting them. The bowl still functions the way a bowl should function, but its beauty and design have changed.

I think God heals us in much the same way. We will never be the versions of ourselves we were before we were hurt, but there is beauty in the cracks. We're not the same, but we're not entirely different either.

※

About a year after we left the church that broke our hearts, it was still difficult for me to attend church services. Everything that was familiar and comfortable about church was also connected to something painful. I was still healing and trying to find Jesus through the fog of the pain. I wasn't sure what I believed anymore, but I was trying to find him.

During this season of sorting, some of our friends planted a church. We made the forty-minute drive to attend a service one Sunday morning, and I lifted my hands in worship for the first time in years.

Zach sat back and watched as I worshiped. He later told me that as my hands were raised, he saw light filling the cracks of my body, which had been broken by someone's reckless, ruthless actions. God was healing me. The parts that were broken would never be the same, but they were being healed and filled with the light of God.

I couldn't see it then because I was still tending to my wounds and leaving a trail of blood behind me wherever I went. Stepping into church was a lot like crossing a field of hidden land mines. It wasn't safe, and it wasn't good. Not yet, anyway. I was still angry, confused, and hurt. I still felt like God had betrayed me. I still wasn't sure if he was who he said he was.

But I wanted to believe. I wanted it to be true. I wanted him to be good. So I worshiped. I poured myself out and hoped he would fix me. I lifted my hands and hoped he would fill them. I turned my eyes toward heaven and hoped I'd see him. I bent my knees and hoped he'd meet me there.

I wasn't looking for answers anymore; I was just tired of being in pain.

One night the disciples were sitting with Jesus, reclining at the table. They might have just finished their meal or they may have still been eating when a woman walked in with a bottle of perfume. None of the records of this event indicate whether she said any words. She simply walked over to Jesus and poured her expensive perfume over his head.

Jesus said that she was doing a beautiful thing and that everywhere the gospel was heard, people would hear about what she'd done. But the disciples just saw a valuable gift being wasted. The perfume could have been used for something else, something better, something more quantifiable. So they asked, "What's the purpose of this waste?"

The disciples couldn't see that what she was doing was a prophetic act of love and worship, preparing Jesus' body for burial and serving as the final catalyst that spurred Judas to betray Jesus. They saw a broken woman wasting wealth. But Jesus didn't see it that way. More than anyone else in that room—even the woman who poured the perfume—Jesus saw it for what it was.*

I wonder who this woman was. I wonder what she'd done to earn the name "sinner." I wonder what Jesus had done to prompt her to respond to his love in such an extravagant way. Her act wasn't a waste. It was the beginning of something new.

I've been the disciples more than I've been the woman with the perfume. I look at things I've gone through and turn my face toward heaven and cry, "For what purpose is this waste, God?"

I've knelt in prayer until my knees were bloody to change the mind of God. When he doesn't, I look at the fragments of my life and wonder how much time I have before God ruins everything again.

I've lived from catastrophe to catastrophe, always anticipating the next one, as if catastrophes are the stepping stones of a good Christian walk.

I find myself relating to Job's response to his friends about what God is doing: "Surely he has now exhausted me."† The English Standard Version reads, "Surely now God has worn me out." With my face on the ground, I wave my white flag and cry, "Enough, God. I've had enough."

---

* Matthew 26:6-13; Luke 7:36-50
† Job 16:7, CSB

We'll do anything to prevent ourselves from hurting again. If we can find the cause, we can find the cure. But there are times we can't find the cause, so we try to make sense of our suffering. Surely there was a point to all this. Maybe there's a lesson to be learned.

We think that if we can pull purpose out of our pain, it will be worth it. Our suffering will have been for something. We can't make peace with a chaotic world that lacks rhyme and reason, so we search for meaning. Surely God wouldn't just waste the pain in our lives.

In his book *Man's Search for Meaning*, Viktor Frankl, a psychiatrist who survived Auschwitz, wrote, "In some ways suffering ceases to be suffering at the moment it finds a meaning."[1]

Without a target, something that's in motion will just keep moving. So what is the target for our suffering? When will our pain hit the thing that makes it stop? We think that if we can find purpose and paint it red, we'll be able to hold the target in front of us. "Here it is!" we'll say to suffering. "Hit this instead of me!"

We think that if we can attach meaning to our heartache, it will give it somewhere to go instead of perpetually tearing us apart, limb by limb. The meaning we give to pain will absorb its sting.

Except it doesn't, really. At least not completely. There are some wounds that will hurt for the rest of your life. Maybe not all the time, but there will be moments when the scar will itch and ache.

The reality is that we are chronically human. We have human bodies. We have human minds. We are subject to those limitations, and outside a supernatural miracle, some wounds won't heal until we are joined with Christ in glory. In order to live our inescapably human lives, we have to make peace with suffering.

The reality is, sometimes our suffering is too great and too heavy to be recycled. We can't reframe it or reshape it into something that doesn't draw blood every time someone gets too close. Some tragedies can't even be spoken out loud. Some breaks are too fragile to handle. And what of those? Are they wasted because they haven't been repurposed? What happens to pain that is never spoken out loud or shared? If the pain is known only by the one who confronts it, is it wasted perfume?

The target of our pain isn't the meaning we can extract from it. It's Jesus.

Regardless of what happened to break our hearts, and regardless of what happens after, our worship isn't in the value of the great things we do with our pain; it's in the act of pouring it out.

The target of our pain isn't the meaning we can extract from it. It's Jesus.

In becoming the target of our pain, Jesus absorbed our suffering for us—not so we could avoid it entirely, but to give us a cure for it. The work of the Cross didn't just create an antidote we get when we die. His death and resurrection give us the freedom to live in abundance, joy, peace, and hope—even while we're still on the earth, even while we still suffer.

We don't have to do mental gymnastics to make sense of things that will likely never make sense to us. We don't have to spend the rest of our lives with no relief from our pain. We have a Savior who is good and kind and trustworthy. In his death, he absorbed our pain. In his resurrection, he conquered it.

There's so much about suffering that we can't know or understand. On this side of the veil, we may never know what the purpose was. But we can be confident that God wastes nothing of our lives. Every drop of our lives is useful and beneficial to the Kingdom of God, because we are his image to the world around us.

The things we go through don't qualify us or promote us, but they do point to the God who is reflected in us. Sure, we can recycle our pain, we can build ministries that change lives, we can raise money for worthy foundations. But our lives aren't measured in what we produce. Our pain doesn't need a purpose to have worth.

Suffering is a bright light that illuminates the path we have no choice but to take. We can't do anything to change what has happened to us, and there's not much we can do to prevent hardship from happening in the future.

We can't make the ache lighter by turning it into something beautiful. Even if we were able to discover the reason it happened or redeem the pain into something useful, the pain will have always happened. The bowl will have always been cracked.

※

We've been misled to believe that God's glory comes only in our victory or that we have control over how his glory plays out. But God's glory is himself. His glory is his glory, and he'll get it no matter what—regardless of how our prayers are answered.

When I was facing the reality of what was happening with our daughters, I wasn't asking myself where God's glory would be found. I believed that I was already surrounded by it. I didn't need a victory to see his glory. I just needed him.

We don't have to tie things up with a pretty bow to make sure we're presenting God in the best light. We don't have to justify our heartbreak to prove that God is still good. We don't have to find a target for it so it will make sense. We don't have to defend God's goodness by dismissing the pain of our experiences.

We can be honest about what we're feeling and experiencing, and it won't dull any of God's glory. He doesn't need our victory to prove himself—he has proven himself already. He's good even when things are bad. He's faithful even when he doesn't answer our prayers. He's merciful even when we don't deserve mercy. He loves us without condition or restriction. The things that happen to us and around us and in us don't change who God is. He's glorified in our suffering and in our victories—not because of the suffering or victories themselves, but because of his unshakable character.

God invites us to be conduits of his glory. When we suffer, when we rejoice, or when our lives are mundane and quiet, we reflect the glory of a good God to the world.

He's glorified in the peace that transcends the darkness of your crisis. He's glorified in the resilience of your faith, even while you're in the fire. He's glorified when things go the way you prayed and you praise him for doing a good thing. He's glorified in your heartbreak as you honor his faithfulness and kindness even when you can't see it or taste it or feel it. He's glorified in the arms you wrap around someone else who's hurting. He's glorified when you offer grace. He's glorified when you tell the truth.

His glory is revealed in you and through you and in spite of you, not in what happens *to* you.

The way you respond to your pain reveals what you believe about God, and it's also an opportunity for greater intimacy with him. Maybe your response to pain will be a beautiful declaration of faith. Maybe it will be an equally beautiful lament of anger and grief. Both are appropriate responses for a righteous person.

When you believe that God is good no matter what, your faith becomes electrifying to everyone in your radius. When you believe that you are safe no matter what, his glory can shine through every fracture of your body and mind.

God is glorified in your tears, in your joy, and in your questions and doubt.

When you're honest about what you're thinking and feeling, however messy and uncomfortable that is to the ears around you, you display a trust and intimacy that many people long to have.

God is glorified in your tears, in your joy, and in your questions and doubt. As you bury dreams, as you lose your faith, as you rebuild it, and as you stand among the fragments of what you thought your life would be, God is glorified in you.

※

In *The Brothers Karamazov*, the classic novel about suffering, Fyodor Dostoyevsky writes, "I believe like a child that suffering will be healed and made up for . . . that in the world's finale, at the moment of eternal harmony, something so precious will come to pass that it will suffice for all hearts, for the comforting of all resentments, for the atonement of all the crimes of humanity, for all the blood that they've shed; that it will make it not only possible to forgive but to justify all that has happened."[2]

It's a beautiful and heartbreaking thought, isn't it? Beautiful to think that there will be a day when the mysteries of earth will collide with a heavenly understanding that makes sense of all the wrongs of this world. But heartbreaking to know that on this side of heaven, we'll just have to be okay with the mysteries. We won't always have the answers, but we don't have to fabricate them either.

There is peace that comes from admitting to yourself and to everyone else that you don't know what you don't know. "I don't know" is a powerful phrase that frees you from leaning on your own understanding.

We don't know. We can't know. We won't know. Until one day, we will.

All suffering is a death of some kind. There are versions of ourselves that die with every heartache. There are aspects of ourselves that are lost forever. There are futures we imagined that we've had to bury and grieve. There are friendships lost, dreams dissolved, marriages ruined, bodies broken, and physical and emotional scars that we will carry forever. It seems almost delusional to believe that anything good could come from what we've lost, and even crazier to believe that good could come *because* of it.

As Jesus was preparing his friends for his death, he said, "The hour has come for the Son of Man to be glorified. Truly I tell you, unless a grain of wheat falls to the ground and dies, it remains by itself. But if it dies, it produces much fruit."* That's the backwards, upside-down, inside-out nature of the Kingdom. In death, we have life. In order to live and grow, we have to die. Our bodies will die once, but our spirits are put to death over and over again as we live and breathe on this side of eternity. Each death brought by suffering is an opportunity for life.

If I'm being honest, I'm happy with the tree I have right now and would like very much for it to not die, even if it means getting new fruit. I don't want the new fruit. I like what we have going already. But there's only one who has the power over life and death, and it isn't me. Sometimes things have to die. But we can still live.

The Christian life has never been about the pursuit of comfort. Some doctrines might promise wealth and health if you follow a certain checklist of good Christian behavior, but those doctrines fail to present the full work of the gospel.

God never said life with him would be easy. But he has promised to be with us every second of it.† When we recognize Jesus as the Son of God, we're acknowledging that there's something a lot bigger than all of us. It's bigger than our whole world. And if it's bigger than the world, than the *universe*, it's without a doubt much bigger than our pain.

But that doesn't mean our pain is insignificant or should be dismissed. It's the opposite, actually! Jesus gave up his throne to become like us so he could be familiar with the suffering we have

---

* *John 12:23-24*, CSB
† *Matthew 28:20*

to endure, so he could be a God who is not only like us but understands us.

One of the most distinctive marks of Christian belief is that God is never ambivalent to our pain. He never treats us like he's too big for us. He loves us and is close to us when we're broken. It's kind of wild, when you think about it—that the God who hung the stars and ordered the earth is close to you when you're hurting. "Who am I that you are mindful of me?"*

The world turns its head toward our response to suffering. People ask questions about our strength and fortitude, not immediately recognizing that it isn't our own strength but Christ at work in us and through us.

God is glorified through every broken piece. We don't need to mask our pain to protect his glory. We don't need to shine a spotlight on our pain either. There's no spiritual edification in elevating and glorifying our suffering—God doesn't need it, and he isn't glorified by it. If we illuminate the suffering, the suffering is all that's seen. Instead, we have an opportunity to illuminate the God who is with us in it.

God is glorified in our sincerity. Our response to pain is the perfume poured out on his feet. Our response might be misunderstood. But it is never wasted. As we surrender the grief over what we've lost and as we trust him with our most fragile aches, God begins to shape new and beautiful things in us and around us. We might have to live in the company of pain, but we also live with the cure for it in us and all around us. Christ is in us, and the presence of God surrounds us, always. We are never apart from him, even in our darkest nights.

Our lives are rivers—constantly in motion, ever changing, always flowing at a different pace. The suffering that comes into

* Psalm 8:4

our lives flows in us and through us, sometimes affecting the course of the water but not changing us completely. The river remains a river, and we hold on to parts of who we are while letting other parts float away. The things that have hurt us won't ruin us. God is glorified in our lives, and we pour ourselves and all our sufferings out for him. As you hold your pain and as your pain holds on to you, as you release it and as you trust the Lord with every piece, you inch closer to being relieved of it forever. But here in the ache of it, you just want to know that God is close and that you're okay.

You *are* okay. And you *will be* okay. That's a promise to look forward to and a truth to grasp right now.

In this moment, when your heart is heavy and you're not sure if the sun will ever shine in your life again, look at the cracks your heartbreak has made in your body. If you look closely enough, you'll see a little light breaking through. Breathe in hope, friend. His light is in you, healing every piece and making you new again. I hope the next breath you take is a little easier. And the next one after that, and the one after that.

※

As I shared the girls' story on social media, I found new community and friendship with men and women who'd had medically complicated experiences. One day I shared about how much I was struggling emotionally, and someone messaged me to say that in her experience, it took about eighteen months after coming home from the NICU before you start to feel normal again. I've found that to be true. I don't know about the science behind it, but somewhere around eighteen months post NICU, I started to breathe again. It took months of therapy and navigating my triggers and processing the rawest of emotions, but my mind and my body healed. We found new rhythms as a family of seven.

When we took our first vacation together, shortly before Chloe and Lydia's second birthday, Zach and I sort of marveled at how far we'd come, not just since the girls were born but from who we were before they were a thought in our minds. Our marriage was stronger and healthier, and we were bonding with our older children in more intentional ways. But perhaps the most notable difference was how much we'd learned to relax. I relaxed into my role as a mother, Zach relaxed into our stage of life, and we both relaxed into the safety of knowing that we are loved by a God who is good and kind and faithful.

There was a shift that happened in our lives and in our relationships (with each other and with God) when we stopped analyzing our faith to make sure it was "right" and began to really trust in the God we believed in. We found peace in a storm, and that peace has remained.

✳

Suffering is a topic that is hotly discussed and thoroughly debated by theologians, philosophers, and anyone who searches for what it means to be human. The phrase "suffer well" has become common in evangelical culture in recent years. I'm not sure who said it first or how it became popular, but it's often used to talk about a Christian response to suffering.

Some people teach that we're called to suffer well to be a model for others. *Set a good example. Don't let doubts take over your mind. Praise God anyway. Be joyful. Be patient. Turn your mourning into dancing. Do everything right so you'll be blessed. Don't cause someone else to fall away.* Others teach that suffering well is proof of our righteousness. The greater the display of faith and boldness in the face of trials, the greater the righteousness. And some teach that suffering well is placing your trust and hope in Christ, without doubts or wavering.

All these perspectives might have elements of truth to them, but they lay the full responsibility of how we endure suffering on the one who's suffering. But as believers in Christ, we aren't called to live in isolation—and we aren't asked to suffer in isolation either. If there is any such thing as suffering well, it's found in the body of Christ's ability to *suffer with*. We don't suffer well alone. We suffer well together.

We aren't capable of containing our pain. It will spill out no matter what we do to prevent it. Unless we face our pain and engage with it in the presence of God, our pain will fester and boil, and infect us and those around us.

Maybe the goal of suffering isn't to suffer well at all, but to *face* suffering well. When we know how loved we are and when we trust that God is good, we can carry our burdens to him with confidence and hope. We can face our heartaches with hope, and because of that hope, we can be joyful, even as our hearts break.

The things that have hurt you are not—and never will be—the end of you. You are changing, even now, and the things that grow will have good and beauty in them, even though they came at a great cost. Like Jacob, you might walk with a limp from this point on,* but that limp is a reminder of all you survived and all God has brought you through.

Don't hide your limp. Don't belittle it either. The limp is proof that what meant to cripple you failed. You stood up again. You walked. You danced.

You suffered. And you survived.

We never asked for the things that hurt us, but we can allow

---

* *Genesis 32*

ourselves to be changed by them. And in that opening of our hearts, we reflect the glory of God to the hurting world around us.

Allowing ourselves to be emotionally honest and spiritually sincere with the God who has permitted our suffering isn't an act of rebellion. Our standing with God has never been dependent on our ability to hide our thoughts and feelings from him. As if we could hide from him anyway! Every time we engage our heart, we move closer to the one who knows us better than we know ourselves. He isn't afraid of our ugliest thoughts. So let's speak them out loud so we can move forward and be free of them.

When you suffer, you're living out your worst-case scenario. When you find yourself in this place, you're wrestling with this horrible reality in an earthly realm while also battling things that are deeply spiritual and intangible. Sometimes it feels like you're being pulled apart, limb by limb. But even when the worst case happens, you are safe.

Even in the worst case, God is still good. Even if life folds in around you, you are loved and held and safe. Even in the worst case, you aren't alone. Even in the worst case, God is good. He is kind. He is faithful. He is just. He is righteous. He is sovereign. He is loving. He is with you. He is in you. He is all around you. You are loved by a good King.

Things might not go the way you prayed. Your body might have failed you, your people might have failed you, your faith might have failed you, but he hasn't. And he won't.

You are safe with Jesus. Even if you can't feel it, there's a beautiful, sacred, holy work happening in you and around you right now, at this very moment. I hope you know how deeply God loves you and how tenderly he holds your heart. And that's true whether you're basking in the joy of answered prayer or grieving in the aftermath of things not turning out the way you hoped and prayed. The goodness and faithfulness of God are on full display when he does for us what we've asked from him, but even if he doesn't, your faith will enable you to say, "He is still good."

Sometimes the circumstances that cause us the deepest pain help us to know God in the deepest ways. When we engage with our pain honestly, we give God the opportunity to heal it completely. When we engage with our questions and our doubts, we accept the invitation to know God better through them. When we feel our emotions without restraint and release them like the perfume from Mary's jar, our deepest hurts are transformed into worship, poured out on the feet of Jesus.

So I don't know about Mr. Skinny Jeans and his "Don't let your circumstances change the way you view God" thing. I say, let them change. Because that change might just bring you closer to understanding that much more how deeply God loves you. Paul wrote* that in order to even begin to understand the height, width, and depth of the love of Christ, we would need to join our comprehension with "all the saints." And even then, Christ's love surpasses all our knowledge.

That's a lot of love to comprehend.

Ephesians 3:18

THE DISTORTION:
My suffering must have a purpose and
a victory that can be seen and measured.

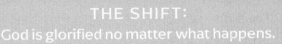

THE SHIFT:
God is glorified no matter what happens.

Acknowledgments

One of the last conversations I had with my grandfather happened around nine years ago. I was sitting on his back porch shortly after giving birth to my third child, sipping sweet tea and chatting about life when he turned to me and asked, "Why aren't you writing anymore?"

I laughed and said, "Oh, I don't know, Papa. I have kids now. I don't really have anything to write about anymore."

He shook his head and adjusted himself in his seat and said, "Now, *Christian.*" (His deep Southern accent never let him pronounce my name the correct way.) "God has given you a gift and anointed you. You need to use the voice he gave you to glorify him."

I thought about what he was saying, but before I could respond, he said, "I have this sermon that I wrote years ago." He told me the story of the sermon, why he wrote it, and the Scripture it was birthed from.

He disappeared inside the house for a few minutes and came back out with a few pages of stapled computer paper. He handed them to me, and I read the title across the top of the first page: "To What Purpose Is This Waste." The sermon was about the woman who poured oil on the feet of Jesus, prompting the disciples to ask each other, "To what purpose is this waste?" As I flipped through his words, he said, "I think you can do something really nice with this."

This book is in your hands because of that backyard conversation all those years ago. After that, I started writing again, working on my craft, telling my story, finding an audience for it, and honoring the "waste" of my life. I can't begin any kind of acknowledgments without first acknowledging my papa. Thank you, Papa, for believing that my words mattered, even when I didn't. Every word I've ever written and will ever write is because you loved me, believed me, challenged me, and helped me center myself every time I lost my way. I miss you every day.

Every writer dreams of having an audience for their words to find a home, and I am so thankful to have found mine. Thank you to every person who has ever read an Instagram caption, a blog post, or a slightly unhinged Instagram story rant. I am so thankful for the ways you've supported my writing. Thank you for loving my family in pain and in joy and in peace. And to the other online communities who adopted my family while we were in crisis, this book is here because you held our arms up when we didn't have the energy to fight. To the Instafamilia and Governerds, I am immeasurably grateful.

Kasey Jackson, my platonic soulmate, you have born witness to the pain in this book and to the pain I may never put into written words in ways that no one else will ever see or know. Thank you for seeing me. Thank you for making me feel safe. And thank you for not deleting my number even though I told you to that one time.

To my parents and siblings, thank you for always encouraging me to write and never trying to silence my voice, even though I know the things I write are hard to read sometimes. Your support has helped me walk boldly and bravely in the call God has given me.

To all the medical staff and NICU doctors and nurses who held my babies and helped me take them home, thank you. It's never lost on me that this story could have had a different ending. Thank you for taking care of us.

Behind every book is an entire team of people making it happen, and I am so thankful for the team that helped me bring these words into the world. To my publishing team, thank you. There's probably no one more fragile than a first-time author who cares way too much about every little thing, but you never made me feel anything less than fully supported.

Zach, my love. An acknowledgment in the back of a book feels kind of ridiculous. You deserve a whole book, and you'd never even ask for a word. Neither one of us knew what kinds of heartbreaks would be waiting for us on the other side of our vows, but I'm so glad you're the one who has been holding my hand all these years. Thank you for being my breath and my laughter, and for bringing me lattes, indulging my food hyper fixations, and supporting every emotionally charged writing session that could only be cured by an immediate dash to Chick-fil-A. You're my best friend and favorite person. Thank you for believing in me, in spite of me constantly trying to convince you not to.

And lastly, to my kids—Jonah, Emery, Anna, Chloe, and Lydia. We have walked through hard things together, and you have been my joy and my pride in every step. I love you so much.

Notes

AUTHOR'S NOTE

1. Elisabeth Elliot, *Suffering Is Never for Nothing* (Nashville: B&H Publishing Group, 2019), 3.

CHAPTER 6: DEEP CRIES TO DEEP

1. Timothy Keller, *Prayer: Experiencing Awe and Intimacy with God* (New York: Penguin, 2016), 18.
2. Augustine, *Confessions* (Oxford: Oxford University Press, 1998), 59.
3. A. W. Tozer, *We Travel an Appointed Way: Making Spiritual Progress* (Chicago: Moody Publishers, 2018), 58.
4. HELPS Word Studies, 2799, "audible weeping," WP, 2, 88, https://biblehub.com/greek/2799.htm.
5. H. R. Jerajani et al., "Hematohidrosis: A Rare Clinical Phenomenon," *Indian Journal of Dermatology* 54, no. 3 (July–September 2009): 290–292, https://www.ncbi.nlm.nih.gov/pmc/articles/PMC2810702/.
6. C. S. Lewis, *A Grief Observed* (New York: HarperOne, 1989), 6.

CHAPTER 8: WHEN JOY LOCKS HANDS WITH GRIEF

1. Ray C. Stedman, "Rejoicing in Suffering," Ray Stedman Ministries, accessed March 10, 2023, https://www.raystedman.org/new-testament/romans/rejoicing-in-suffering.

CHAPTER 9: THE SACREDNESS OF SHARED PAIN

1. These ancient religions have been studied extensively by both Christian and non-Christian historians. The secular perspective is that the Christian God is another one of these mythical gods. The Christian perspective is that the story of God and his people was written, recorded, and shared in

a specific way *because* there were so many gods and religions with similar components. God is the true God, Jesus the true Son, Christ the only way, his power the only true power. The major difference between Christianity and other religions is that Jesus was an actual historical person. We know that he existed. This is quite the academic undertaking, but if you're of a curious mind, start with Dr. Pat Zukeran, who leads Evidence and Answers, a Christian apologetics ministry.

2. Kyle Harper, "Solving the Mystery of an Ancient Roman Plague," *Atlantic*, November 1, 2017, https://www.theatlantic.com/science/archive/2017/11/solving-the-mystery-of-an-ancient-roman-plague/543528/.

3. Eusebius, *The History of the Church*, trans. G. A. Williamson (New York: Penguin Books, 1989), 237.

4. Jennie A. McLaurin and Cymbeline Tancongco Culiat, *Designed to Heal: What the Body Shows Us about Healing Wounds, Repairing Relationships, and Restoring Community* (Carol Stream, IL: Tyndale, 2021), 46.

5. This concept and the neuroscience of being "glad to be together" is explored more thoroughly in Chris M. Coursey, *Transforming Fellowship: 19 Brain Skills That Build Joyful Community* (East Peoria, IL: Shepherd's House, 2016).

CHAPTER 10: THE GLORY AROUND US

1. Viktor E. Frankl, *Man's Search for Meaning*, trans. Ilse Lasch (Boston: Beacon Press, 2006), 113.

2. Fyodor Dostoyevsky, *The Brothers Karamazov* (New York: Bantam Dell, 1970), 313.

About the Author

Kristen LaValley is a writer and storyteller whose words offer a refreshing perspective on faith and spirituality and resonate with those who carry tension in their faith. She offers insights that intersect doubt and belief, hope and suffering, beauty and heartache. With a deep love for the Christian faith and a willingness to explore its complexities, Kristen's writing offers nuanced conversations that challenge readers to think deeply and wrestle with important questions. Kristen lives in Massachusetts with her husband, Zach, and their five children.

Online Discussion *guide*

Take *your* Tyndale reading
Experience *to the* Next Level

A FREE discussion guide for this book
is available at bookclubhub.net, perfect
for sparking conversations in your book
group or for digging deeper into the text
on your own.

www.bookclubhub.net

*You'll also find free discussion guides for
other Tyndale books, e-newsletters, e-mail
devotionals, virtual book tours, and more!*